Accounting and Tax Aspects of Franchising

The Little, Brown Tax Advisory Board

THE LITTLE, BROWN TAX PRACTICE SERIES

Accounting and Tax Aspects of Franchising

1995 Edition

Bruce S. Schaeffer
Member, New York Bar

John L. Allbery
Deloitte & Touche LLP, Des Moines

This volume is current through April 15, 1995.

Little, Brown and Company
Boston New York Toronto London

Library of Congress Catalog No. 95-77104
ISBN 0-316-77298-4

ICP

Published simultaneously in Canada
by Little, Brown & Company (Canada) Limited

Printed in the United States of America

Summary of Contents

Contents	vii
About the Authors	xiii
Acknowledgments	xv
Introduction	xvii
1 The Franchise Industry and Its Legal Environment	1
2 Overview of Structuring Options for Franchise Relationships	13
3 Franchise Transfers and Retransfers	21
4 Multiple-Unit Transactions	47
5 Pooled Advertising Funds	53
6 Passive "Royalty" Income: Personal Holding Company and S Corporation Considerations	63
7 State and Local Income Tax "Nexus"	79
8 State Sales and Use Tax "Nexus"	93
9 International Franchising and Licensing Tax Considerations	99
10 Other Services to Franchisees and Tax Planning Considerations for the Franchisor	111
11 Succession Planning for Franchisees	117
Appendix Alternative Minimum Tax—Book Income Preferences	129
Table of Cases	133
Table of Internal Revenue Code Sections	135
Table of Treasury Regulations	137
Table of Treasury Rulings	139
Table of Miscellaneous Rulings	141
Table of Secondary Authorities	143
Index	145

Contents

About the Authors xiii
Acknowledgments xv
Introduction xvii

1

The Franchise Industry and Its Legal Environment 1

§101 Types of Franchise Arrangements 1
§102 History and Development 2
§103 The Economics of a Franchise 3
§104 Franchising in the 1990s 4
§105 International Franchising 6
§106 Regulation of Franchise Sales and Disclosure 8
§106.1 The FTC Franchise Disclosure Rule 8
§106.2 State Regulatory Activity 9
§107 Franchise Company Mergers and Acquisitions 11

2

Overview of Structuring Options for Franchise Relationships 13

§201 Franchise Arrangements, Generally 13
§202 Initial Franchise Fees 15
§202.1 Intangibles (Including Protection Radius) 15
§202.2 Site Selection and Approval 16
§203 Royalties, License Fees, or Service Fees 16
§204 Additional Services 17
§205 Transfer Fees 17
§206 Master Licensees 17
§206.1 Territorial Agreements 17
§206.2 Development Schedules 18
§207 Advertising Funds 19

3

Franchise Transfers and Retransfers 21

§301 Franchise Transfers, Generally 22
§302 Legislative History 23
§303 Characterization and Recognition of Receipts by the Franchisor 24
§303.1 Initial Franchise Fees 25
§303.2 Royalties, License Fees, or Service Fees 26
§303.3 Master License Fees 26
§303.4 Subsequent Transfer Fees 26
§304 Deductibility of Franchise Costs by Franchisees 26
§304.1 Initial Franchise Fees 27
§304.1.1 Prior Law 27
§304.1.2 Current Law—Present Cost of Acquisitions—Amortizable Franchise Fee 28
§304.2 Present Discounted Value of Right to Deduct Initial Franchise Fee 29
§304.3 Master License Fees 30
§304.4 Subsequent Transfer Fees 30
§305 Different Treatment of Franchisor and Franchisee 30
§306 A Modest Proposal—The Overriding Royalty 32
§307 Unbundling of Initial Franchise Fees 34
§308 Purchases of Existing Franchise Operations at a Premium: Goodwill or Franchise Rights? 35
§309 *Canterbury v. Commissioner* 36
§309.1 Introduction 36
§309.2 Goodwill and Going-Concern Value 37
§309.2.1 Goodwill in the Normal Business Context 37
§309.2.2 In the Normal Franchise Context 38
§309.2.3 The Unique McDonald's Facts 39
§309.3 The IRS Arguments in *Canterbury* 41
§309.3.1 Franchisor's "Franchisee Fee" for New Franchises Establishes Amount That Can Be Amortized as "Franchise Fee" 41
§309.3.2 Purchaser of Operating Franchise May Not Amortize Amount as a Franchise Fee Greater Than Amount Original Franchisee Paid 41
§309.3.3 Purchaser of Operating Franchise Acquires Other Nonamortizable Assets Such as Goodwill and Large Portion of Purchase Price Should Be Allocated to Those Intangibles 42

§310 Code §1060 Requirements Regarding Transfers and Retransfers 43
§310.1 Legislative History of Code §1060 43
§310.2 Allocation of Consideration Under the Residual Method 44
§310.3 Required Reporting and Compliance 45

4

Multiple-Unit Transactions 47

§401 Multiple-Unit Transactions, Generally 47
§402 Subfranchising Arrangements 48
§402.1 Legal and Regulatory Aspects 48
§402.2 Tax Accounting 48
§402.3 Financial Accounting 48
§403 Area Development Agreements 49
§403.1 Legal and Regulatory Aspects 49
§403.2 Tax Accounting 50
§403.3 Financial Accounting 50
§404 Area Representative Agreements 51
§404.1 Legal and Regulatory Aspects 51
§404.2 Tax Accounting 51
§404.3 Financial Accounting 51
§405 Brokers 52
§405.1 Legal and Regulatory Aspects 52
§405.2 Tax Accounting 52
§405.3 Financial Accounting 52

5

Pooled Advertising Funds 53

§501 Purpose of the Funds 53
§502 IRS Position 54
§502.1 The Seven-Up Company 54
§502.2 *Ford Dealers Advertising Fund Co.*—The Issue Resurrected 55
§502.3 Nonacquiescence: Revenue Rulings 74-318, 74-319 55
§502.4 Continued Litigation—*Insty-Prints,* etc. 56
§503 Tax Status of the Fund 56
§503.1 Form of the Fund Entity 57
§503.2 Is the Fund a Separate Taxpayer? 59

§504 Payments to the Fund 59
§504.1 Are Payments to the Fund Income for Tax Purposes? 59
§504.2 Are Payments Deductible for Tax Purposes? 60
§505 Planning Considerations 60
§506 Alternative Defense 62
§507 Conclusion 62

6

Passive "Royalty" Income: Personal Holding Company and S Corporation Considerations 63

§601 Passive "Royalty" Income, Generally 63
§602 Personal Holding Companies 63
§602.1 Statutory Requirements 65
§602.2 Legislative Purpose and History 66
§602.3 Case Law—Franchising 68
§602.4 Case Law—"Compensation for Services" versus "Royalty Income" 69
§602.5 Recommendations 71
§603 S Corporations 74

7

State and Local Income Tax "Nexus" 79

§701 Background 79
§702 Due Process 80
§703 Commerce Clause 80
§704 New York 81
§704.1 "Doing Business" 81
§704.2 Jurisdiction 81
§704.3 "Employing Capital" 85
§704.4 "Allocation Formula" 87
§705 New Mexico 88
§705.1 "Engaging in Business" 89
§705.2 "Leasing Property" 90
§706 South Carolina 90
§707 Multistate Tax Commission 92
§708 Conclusion 92

8

State Sales and Use Tax "Nexus" 93

§801 Overview 93
§802 State Sales and Use Tax Nexus 94
§803 *National Bellas Hess, Inc. v. Illinois Department of Revenue* 95
§804 Special Problems Facing the Franchise Industry 96
§804.1 Services 97
§804.2 Franchise Fees 97
§805 Taxable Components of Fees Paid Under Franchising Arrangements 97
§806 Summary 98

9

International Franchising and Licensing Tax Considerations 99

§901 International Franchising, Generally 99
§902 Structuring Franchise Relationships 100
§902.1 "Super-Royalty" Provisions and Excise Tax ("Toll Charge") on Transfers to Foreign Entities 100
§903 Franchisor Directly Licenses Franchises to Unrelated Foreign Franchisees 102
§903.1 Treaties with the United States 102
§903.2 Withholding and Other Taxes Imposed on Franchise Fees 102
§903.3 Foreign Tax Credit 103
§904 Franchisor Licenses (or Sells) Franchises to Foreign Subsidiary or Other Related Party Who Sublicenses (or Licenses) to Unrelated Foreign Franchisees 105
§904.1 Franchise Fees Characterized as Active or Passive Income 106
§905 Franchisor Licenses (or Sells) Franchises Through Territorial Master Licensees Who Then Sublicense (or License) the Franchises to Foreign Franchisees Unrelated to the Franchisor or the Master Licensee 107
§906 Franchising Versus Licensing 107
§907 Planning for International Licensing and Royalty Flow 108
§908 Licensing and Technical Support 109
§909 Summary 109

10

Other Services to Franchisees and Tax Planning Considerations for the Franchisor 111

§1001 Tax Planning Considerations, Generally 111
§1002 Targeted Jobs Tax Credit Programs 111
§1003 Ad Valorem Tax Studies 112
§1004 Franchisor-Sponsored Retirement Programs for Franchise Owners 113
§1005 ZEESOP or ZSOP Plans 113
§1006 Accounting Methods and Periods 115
§1007 Uniform Capitalization of Inventory Costs 115
§1008 "Passive" Losses from Royalty Arrangements 115
§1009 Affiliated Company Considerations and Elections 115

11

Succession Planning for Franchisees 117

§1101 Succession Planning, Generally 117
§1102 Restrictions on Transfer 118
§1103 Permission to Transfer 120
§1104 Transfers to a Spouse—Overfunding the Marital Share 121
§1105 Valuation 122
§1105.1 Empirical Studies 123
§1105.2 Statutory Changes 124
§1105.3 Case Law 125
§1106 Potential Income Tax Liabilities 127
§1107 Availability of Code §6166 127

Appendix Alternative Minimum Tax—Book Income Preferences 129

Table of Cases 133
Table of Internal Revenue Code Sections 135
Table of Treasury Regulations 137
Table of Treasury Rulings 139
Table of Miscellaneous Rulings 141
Table of Secondary Authorities 143
Index 145

About the Authors

John L. Allbery, CPA, is the Office Managing Partner for the Des Moines office of Deloitte & Touche LLP. The areas of emphasis in his practice are franchising, manufacturing, wholesaling and retail, real estate, closely-held businesses, and personal financial planning. He is also the Director of Franchise Industry Services for the Firm. Allbery holds a Bachelor of Arts degree in accounting from Doane College and a Master of Business Administration in taxation from Golden Gate University. He has been a speaker on franchising at numerous functions for clients, professional accounting organizations and franchise trade-industry groups. Allbery is also actively involved in several professional activities dedicated to franchise organizations. He has served on the International Franchise Association's Board of Directors, Long-Range Planning Committee, Legal/Legislative Committee, and is the past Chairman of the Council of Franchise Suppliers. He also serves on the Franchise Advisory Board for the University of St. Thomas in Minneapolis, and on the Executive Advisory Board of the International Center for Franchise Studies at the University of Nebraska-Lincoln. For the last several years, Allbery has spent a significant amount of time dealing with the federal and state tax considerations of franchising. He has developed many innovative and cost-effective planning strategies for franchise companies and has been involved in numerous sales, acquisitions, and leveraged buyouts of franchise businesses. In addition to significant local franchise client responsibilities, he has been involved in many national franchise consulting projects for Deloitte & Touche LLP.

Bruce S. Schaeffer, Esq., is an attorney in private practice with offices at 404 Park Avenue South, New York, New York. He concentrates his practice in the areas of estate planning, franchising and securities fraud.

Mr. Schaeffer holds a Master of Laws (in Taxation) from New York University School of Law and a Juris Doctor degree from Brooklyn Law School. Among his publications are "Maximum Marital Deduction Clause Not Always the Best Choice," Estate Planning, 1978; "Reasonable Compensation and Accumulated Earnings," New York University 39th Annual Institute on Federal Taxation, 1981; "Tax Planning To Avoid The Accumulated Earnings Tax," The Practical Accountant, 1982; "Reasonable Compensation: Defending Against an IRS Attack," The Practical Accountant, 1982; "Avoiding The State Death Tax Disadvantages of the Unlimited Marital Deduction in Large Estates," Estate Planning, 1983; "Rehabilitation Tax Credit—The 'Substantial Rehabilitation' Test," Tax Management Real Estate Journal, 1985; "Franchises Fee Collection: Reaping the Benefits of Franchise Tax Deductions," Franchise Legal Digest, 1985; "Success Problems and the Closely Held Franchisor—The Personal Holding Company Tax," Franchise Legal Digest,

1986; "Estate Planning for Franchises" Taxation for Accountants, 1989; "The Cost of Acquisition of Franchises—Canterbury v. Commissioner" Business Franchise Guide, 1992.

Mr. Schaeffer has lectured for the New York University Institute on Federal Taxation, Franchise Legal Symposium, the Practicing Law Institute and many other symposia. Mr. Schaeffer is an occasional lecturer at Brooklyn Law School and was formerly the co-author of the CCH Tax Transactions Library Volume on Franchising. He served for many years as a member of the International Franchise Association's Finance Accounting and Tax Committee and is currently a member of the Legal/Legislative Committee of the IFA.

Acknowledgments

We are indebted to Dwayne Vande Krol of Deloitte & Touche LLP in Des Moines, Iowa, for his assistance with respect to the chapter on State and Local Income Tax "Nexus," Russel Greenstein, CPA, of Arthur Andersen, New York, New York, for his review and additions to the chapter on State and Local Sales and Use Tax "Nexus," and Pat Hoyt of Deloitte & Touche LLP in Des Moines, Iowa, and Michelle Harris in New York, New York, for their aid in preparing the manuscript for printing.

Introduction

§1 FRANCHISING, IN GENERAL

Franchising is a method of doing business in which the franchisor's know-how and good name are coupled with the franchisee's hard work and equity. The word "franchise" literally means to be free. Franchising provides countless entrepreneurs the freedom to own, manage, and direct their own businesses. In franchising, the franchisor is the party that owns the rights to the trademark, trade name, and/or system of doing business. The franchisee is the one who purchases the right to use these assets.

The history of franchising can be traced to the pre-Civil War era, beginning with the Singer Sewing Machine Company and the advent of brewers' licensing of beer gardens to independent parties to expand distribution. Although franchising began over a century ago, many tax issues unique to businesses employing the franchise concept are frequently not clearly understood by the franchisor, the franchisees, or their advisers.

The franchise system is a significant part of the U.S. economy, annually creating business opportunities, jobs, entrepreneurs, and services as well as export opportunities. Franchising has been called the last and best hope for independent business in an era of growing vertical integration. It helps small businesses compete with the giants because franchisees have a good chance to survive and prosper using the franchisor's know-how and trademark or service mark. In addition, a franchisee's survival chances are enhanced through operating efficiencies provided by bulk buying discounts, shared advertising funds, decreased overhead costs, and reduced demand for experienced personnel and associated payroll costs. Franchising also offers a unique opportunity to people with limited capital and experience.

From the franchisor's standpoint, large outlays of capital to expand the markets for products or services are often avoided through the use of the franchise concept. Franchise systems have provided a means for many businesses to expand quickly without diminishing the quality of products or services. Franchising also has provided the opportunity for businesses with limited resources to achieve nationwide distribution and recognition of their products or services with minimal outlay of their own capital.

According to the most current statistics from *Franchising in the Economy, 1988-1990*, a publication of the International Franchise Association Educational Foundation, Inc., and Horwath International, franchising sales of goods and services in nearly 600,000 outlets were expected to reach almost $800 billion in 1992, more than double the level of sales at the start of the 1980s. Employment in franchising, including part-time workers and working proprietors, was 7 million in 1987 and was expected to increase to more than 8 million by the end of 1992. Retail sales generated by franchise establishments already account for more than one-third of all retail sales in the United States. This level may increase from 40.9 percent in 1992 to 50 percent near the turn of the century.

Franchising is used by companies active in nearly 100 types of business enterprises. The U.S. Department of Commerce calls franchising a "significant part of the U.S. economy" and reports that franchising "continues to prove its validity as a marketing method adaptable to an ever-widening array of industries and professions while providing immediate identity and recognition for prospective entrepreneurs joining the system."

Essentially, there are two kinds of franchising arrangements: product/trade name franchising (product distribution arrangements in which the dealer is, to some degree but not entirely, identified with the manufacturer or supplier) and business format franchising. Typical of product/trade name franchising are automobile and truck dealerships, gasoline service stations, and soft drink bottlers. These three industries accounted for 71 percent of franchise sales in 1987.

In business format franchising, the franchisor establishes a fully integrated relationship with the franchise owner, governing the product or service, trademark, marketing strategy, standards, and quality control. Business format franchises offer the franchise owner not only the use of trademarks, trade names, and so on, but a complete system of doing business. The term "system" is the key concept in business format franchising. The franchisor provides a complete operations manual and establishes communications and support systems for franchisees.

Although a number of outlets in the product/trade name category have declined in recent years, business format franchising experienced consistent unit growth for over 20 years.

The expansion of franchising into a broad range of retail and service industries—including automotive products and services, lodging, restaurants, rentals, business aids and services, food and nonfood retailing, educational and health activities, home care, travel, and recreation—is gradually changing the traditional marketing system for consumer goods and services. At the same time, franchising continues to offer opportunities for those individuals seeking to own businesses. Utilizing current marketing techniques, franchisors are able to keep pace with shifting consumer markets and offer management expertise and market-resource assistance to potential entrepreneurs.

Franchising is viewed by the Department of Commerce as a dynamic, growing business activity increasingly accepted and respected by the public, all levels of government, and the business community. Franchising has become a powerful force, in part, because economic factors have made growth through company-owned units difficult for many businesses. By emphasizing independent ownership, franchising provides an effective method of overcoming such problems as shortage of capital, high interest rates, and hiring and keeping competent employees.

§2 BUSINESS FORMAT FRANCHISING

The most popular franchise is the "business format" franchise (auto dealerships, gas stations, and bottling companies are considered franchises by the Department of Commerce but are subject to different legal requirements). A business format franchise generally has three elements: (1) a trademark, (2) a business plan or system of operation, and (3) the payment of fees usually consisting of an initial franchise fee in a fixed amount and an ongoing payment based on operations, usually described as a royalty, license fee, or service fee.

Business format franchising is characterized by an ongoing business relationship between franchisor and franchisee that includes not only the product, service, and trademark but also the entire business format itself: a marketing strategy and plan, operating manuals and standards, quality control, and continuing two-way communications. Restaurants, nonfood retailing, personal and business services, rental services, real estate services, and other service businesses fall into the category of business format franchising. Business format franchises have been responsible for much of the growth of franchising in the United States since 1950 and will continue to offer opportunities for those individuals seeking their own businesses.

With the continuing shift in the domestic economy from the manufacturing to the service sectors and the proliferation of two-income families, business format franchising is entering new fields. Among the fastest-growing franchising ventures are residential cleaning services, home repairs and remodeling, carryout restaurants, quick lube and oil change centers, auto tune-up and detailing, personnel and temporary agencies, weight control centers, hair salons, and miscellaneous business services, including printing and copying, accounting, tax preparation, and computer and software sales.

There are also trends within business format franchising itself: independent businesses are "converting" to franchising (especially in the real estate and travel industries). In addition, franchisors are seeking multiunit or "master" franchisees and combination franchises under one roof.

The volume of sales and the number of units owned or franchised by business format franchisors has been rising steadily since 1972. Sales of business format franchisors were nearly $214 billion in 1990, compared with $192 billion in 1989 and $178 billion in 1988. The number of establishments of business format franchisors increased to almost 393,000 in 1990, compared to 358,000 in 1989 and 339,000 in 1988. The number of establishments and the gross sales of business format franchisors for 1972-1990 (the most current statistics available) are listed below:

Year	*Sales (billions of dollars)*	*Establishments*
1972	28.7	189,640
1973	32.7	202,237
1974	37.3	209,727
1975	40.9	210,814
1976	46.6	222,317

Year	Sales (billions of dollars)	Establishments
1977	65.8	240,524
1978	64.3	245,694
1979	72.4	252,702
1980	83.5	252,548
1981	89.1	260,555
1982	99.0	268,306
1983	110.5	276,195
1984	122.3	283,675
1985	141.3	301,689
1986	155.5	312,810
1987	169.6	334,516
1988	178.3	338,979
1989*	192.4	358,350
1990*	213.2	392,854

*Estimated
†*Source:* U.S. Department of Commerce.

The number of business format franchisors offering their products and/or services to prospective franchisees also has been rising steadily since 1972. This upward trend is expected to continue for the remainder of the century as more and more companies choose to expand their distribution of goods and services through franchising. Listed below are the number of business format franchisors that responded to the Department of Commerce surveys for the period 1972-1988.

Year	Number of Franchisors
1972	909
1973	1,005
1974	1,051
1975	1,115
1976	1,161
1977	1,281
1978	1,394
1979	1,459
1980	1,584
1981	1,673
1982	1,770
1983	1,877
1984	1,942
1985	2,090
1986	2,177
1987*	—
1988	2,239

*No survey conducted.
†*Source:* U.S. Department of Commerce.

Large franchisors, those with 1,000 or more units each, continue to dominate business format franchising, with 69 companies accounting for 51.7 percent of all sales and 53.2 percent of all establishments in 1988. The total number of outlets reported by these large franchisors stood at 180,200, with sales of $92.2 billion in 1988. Sixteen of these large franchisors were engaged in restaurants and eight were in automotive products and services.

§3 RETAILING: DOMINANT IN FRANCHISING

Retailing dominates franchising, accounting for 87 percent of all franchising receipts in 1986. The retail sales of all firms associated with franchising reached about $487 billion in 1986, or 33 percent of all U.S. retail sales, estimated at $1.5 trillion.[1]

Franchise retail sales continue to remain strong as a result of moderate inflation and steady economic growth. Increased application of existing technology to retailing is continuing but with no new breakthroughs. Categories that show stronger than average growth include building materials and hardware, apparel and accessories, furniture and home furnishings, and related items. It is expected that periods of low interest rates and low energy and gasoline prices will contribute to increased retail sales.

§4 THE STABILITY AND SUCCESS OF THE FRANCHISING SYSTEM

The failure rate of franchise companies is extremely low. The number of individually owned franchise outlets discontinued annually for reasons including business failure is also extremely low. According to figures gathered by the Department of Commerce from 1971 to 1987, less than 5 percent of all business format franchisees were discontinued annually.

Renewal rates of franchise contracts are high. For example, 93 percent of franchisor-franchisee contracts were renewed in 1986. The small number of terminations was mostly initiated by the franchisee or by mutual agreement as opposed to terminations by the franchisor.

Virtually all franchisee requests to transfer franchises are approved. Of 4,202 franchisees who sought permission to sell in 1986, all but 94 were approved.

Finally, 94 percent of franchise owners say that they are successful based on a nationwide Gallup survey conducted in 1991; 75 percent of franchisees would repeat their franchise experience again, whereas only 39 percent of Americans surveyed would repeat their current job or business.

§3 [1]U.S. Department of Commerce.

§5 FRANCHISE REGULATION

In much the same way that securities regulation grew out of perceived securities fraud, franchise regulation grew primarily out of perceived franchise fraud.

Futuristic Foods, Holiday Magic, and other purported franchise investments turned out to be schemes to defraud. In response to such schemes, California passed the first franchise law in 1971.[1] Since then, 13 other states have enacted laws adopting the franchise registration and prospectus disclosure requirements pioneered by California: Hawaii, Illinois, Maryland, Michigan, Minnesota, New York, North Dakota, Oregon, Rhode Island, South Dakota, Virginia, Washington, and Wisconsin.

In addition, 19 states have enacted laws that seek to protect franchisees from arbitrary termination or nonrenewal: Arkansas, California, Connecticut, Delaware, Hawaii, Illinois, Indiana, Kentucky, Louisiana, Michigan, Minnesota, Mississippi, Missouri, Nebraska, New Jersey, South Dakota, Virginia, Washington, and Wisconsin.

The Federal Trade Commission's Franchise Rule (FTC Rule) went into effect in 1979.[2] Under the FTC Rule, franchisors must make full presale disclosure nationwide in a prospectus which follows the format set out in the Federal Trade Commission's *Compliance Guide.* The FTC Rule does not generally preempt state legislation. However, franchising can be subject to many, often conflicting, layers of regulations.

§6 CRITICAL FRANCHISING ISSUES

§6.1 Introduction

Franchising is often referred to as a distribution system or method of retailing. It is not an industry. Nonetheless, business format franchising does present some common and unique tax aspects, which would otherwise be referred to as industry specific.

Any commercial enterprise is subject to numerous federal, state, and local tax rules and regulations. The franchise industry is affected by such basic issues as the following: (1) Who is the taxpayer? (2) What is the income? and (3) How does the taxpayer time income and deductions? However, this volume addresses certain tax aspects that are, for the most part, unique to franchising.

§6.2 Importance of Tax Planning

Careful tax planning is critical for the successful operation of a franchise organization, for the transactions in which it engages, and for the organizational struc-

§5 [1]California Regulation and Disclosure Act, Cal. Corp. Code §§31000 et seq.

[2]Disclosure Requirements and Prohibitions Concerning Franchising and Business Opportunity Venture, 16 C.F.R. §436.

tures it creates. There are many pitfalls unique to the federal taxation of franchisors. Furthermore, state and local governments are actively and liberally enforcing their taxing statutes to subsidize their revenue shortfalls created by cutbacks in federal assistance. The application of these federal, state, and local tax laws to the franchise industry requires franchising executives and their advisers to recognize and address the tax considerations of each transaction as a fundamental part of the initial planning for the transaction.

§6.3 *Entity Planning*

The initial tax inquiry as to what form of entity to use to conduct the enterprise is not so much unique to franchising as to the specific facts of the individual transactions. Selecting among the choices—sole proprietorship, partnership, limited partnership, C corporation, S corporation, or some other form of trust or joint venture—is often determined by the specific business, the type of assets involved, the number and business form of the parties involved, and whether the business is publicly or privately held, as well as a variety of other factors. For the most part, business and regulatory factors often outweigh tax factors in determining what sort of entity should be used in franchising.

§6.4 *Structuring the Franchise Relationship and Agreements*

The franchisor has a host of structuring options for franchise arrangement relationships and can make a profit in a number of ways. The arrangements and agreements within a franchise system can differ significantly from one franchise to another based on a number of factors including the nature of the business, the type of franchising considered most appropriate, the need for capital, the amount of services to be provided to franchisees, and the need for structured, systemwide advertising. Chapter 2 is dedicated to an overview of these structuring options.

§6.5 *Franchise Transfers and Retransfers*

The transfers of most franchises are treated under the specific rules of Internal Revenue Code §1253, which makes clear that the transfer of a franchise is unique for tax purposes and is not treated like other business transfers. The current tax factors to be considered in determining the terms and conditions of franchise transfers and retransfers, as well as the different tax treatment accorded the transferor and the transferee, are addressed in Chapter 3. The special rules regarding these transfers will be reviewed in detail. The discussion addresses the recognition of various franchise fees by the franchisor and the deductibility of franchise costs by the franchisee.

§6.6 *Multiple-Unit Transactions*

Multiple-unit transactions take four basic forms: (1) subfranchising, (2) area development agreements, (3) area representative agreements, and (4) franchise brokers. The various legal and regulatory aspects and the tax accounting and financial accounting issues are discussed in Chapter 4.

§6.7 *Pooled Advertising Funds*

Advertising, primarily systemwide and uniform, often lies at the heart of a successful franchise operation. Chapter 5, concerning pooled advertising funds, addresses the tax issues that are unique to the common funding of these campaigns as well as the tortured but uncompromising history of Internal Revenue Service (IRS) defeats in its attempts to tax pooled advertising funds.

§6.8 *Definition of Franchise "Royalties" and Implications for Federal Income Tax Purposes*

Franchisors are likely to label the contingent payments they receive from operations of their franchisees "royalties." In tax law, revenues that are labeled "royalties" can subject the recipient to tax penalties. Chapter 6, concerning passive income, addresses the personal holding company tax, a penalty tax imposed on certain closely held corporations that receive more than the threshold percentage of certain types of "passive" income. Chapter 6 also discusses the tax ramifications of having a franchisor's royalties deemed "passive investment income" for subchapter S purposes.

§6.9 *State and Local Income Tax "Nexus"*

In Chapter 7, the state and local income tax "nexus" is another facet of the passive versus active distinction that addresses the level of activity by a foreign corporate franchisor that will be subject to tax in a state in which its franchisees operate and, conversely, the activity that is permitted without being subject to tax. As federal assistance to states has diminished, state governments are beginning to explore these areas to expand their tax base.

§6.10 *State and Local Sales and Use Tax Considerations*

As with the area of state and local income tax nexus, many state and local governments are liberalizing their interpretations and implementing strict enforcement programs for sales and use taxes. Chapter 8 is dedicated to these issues and includes examples of multistate differences in taxing specific products, transfer pricing issues, breakage rules, and taxation on the resale of existing franchises.

§6.11 *International Franchising*

Many of the international tax considerations for franchising are addressed in Chapter 9. Chapter 9 provides an overview of the basic issues to be reviewed, including the proper form of franchise transfers, the characterization of income received under the franchise arrangements, the resulting foreign and domestic income taxes, and foreign tax credits, registration taxes, value-added taxes, local taxes, employee taxes and/or customs taxes on the income earned under the franchise agreement and related sales of goods and services.

§6.12 *Franchisee Services from the Franchisor*

In Chapter 10, there is a brief discussion of numerous general tax-planning considerations for franchisors and several specific services that can be provided to franchisees. Many of these ideas are unique to franchising.

§6.13 *Succession Planning for Franchise Owners*

Finally, Chapter 11 addresses the issue of succession planning for franchisees. This chapter highlights the importance of the need for the accountant, attorney, and other more traditional estate planners to work closely with the franchisor in developing a succession plan for the franchise-business owner. Due to the unique nature of the franchise asset and potential restrictions on a transfer or an assignment of the franchise in certain situations, a perfectly designed estate plan may be worthless without the cooperation of the franchisor.

§6.14 *Other Planning Considerations*

Many other issues have also been addressed throughout this volume. Problems and opportunities unique to the franchise industry are the timing for recognition of income for tax purposes, as opposed to the timing for financial reporting purposes (and the possibility of the alternative minimum tax being applied with respect to the "book income" preference), the possible application of Code §1060 and its associated compliance requirements, and multiple unit transactions taken into account in accordance with Statement of Financial Accounting Standards No. 45 and the Securities and Exchange Commission guidelines.

§6.15 *Franchise Company Mergers and Acquisitions*

Mergers, acquisitions, and the resulting reorganizations are highly technical and complex in nature so the scope of discussion will be limited (see §107 below).[1] Mergers and acquisitions of franchise businesses do not differ significantly from other business combinations from a tax perspective. However, there are many business and operational differences that are unique to franchise company mergers and acquisitions. Among these differences are franchise regulatory rules, legal and fiduciary duty issues, and geographic exclusivity considerations. These concerns will not be addressed in this volume because they are outside the tax arena. Of course, prior to completing such a transaction, proper legal counsel and franchise consultants specializing in these areas should be consulted to address these unique franchising issues.

§6 [1]For a detailed discussion of mergers and acquisitions, see Ginsburg & Levin, Mergers, Acquisitions, and Buyouts: Transactional Analysis (The Little, Brown Tax Practice Series Jan. 1995).

Accounting and Tax Aspects of Franchising

1

The Franchise Industry and Its Legal Environment

§101 Types of Franchise Arrangements
§102 History and Development
§103 The Economics of a Franchise
§104 Franchising in the 1990s
§105 International Franchising
§106 Regulation of Franchise Sales and Disclosure
§106.1 The FTC Franchise Disclosure Rule
§106.2 State Regulatory Activity
§107 Franchise Company Mergers and Acquisitions

§101 TYPES OF FRANCHISE ARRANGEMENTS

Franchising encompasses a variety of business arrangements which generally fall within two categories: product and trade name franchises and business format franchises. Product and trade name franchises include arrangements in which franchisees are granted the right to distribute manufacturers' products within a specified territory or at a specific location, generally with the use of the manufacturer's identifying name or trademark.

Examples of product/trade name franchises include automobile dealerships, gasoline service stations, soft drink bottlers, and farm equipment dealers. Until the mid-1970s, gasoline stations epitomized the typical business franchise. In 1972, 181,167 gasoline franchises accounted for 80 percent of all gasoline stations, 84 percent of all product franchises, and nearly half (48.6 percent) of all franchise businesses. The oil shocks of the 1970s, together with significant changes within the oil industry in general, reduced the number of gasoline franchises by half. The 91,840 gasoline franchises operating in 1988 still accounted for 82 percent of all gasoline stations and 76 percent of all product franchises, but their share of total franchising declined to 22 percent. Although product/trade name franchises continue to account for two-thirds of all franchise sales, they now represent less than 30 percent of all franchise businesses.[1]

§101 [1]Report of House Committee on Small Business, Franchising in the U.S. Economy: Prospects and Problems (U.S. Department of Commerce, Aug. 13, 1990), at 3.

The business format franchise is a newer development that generally incorporates trademark licensing with the conveyance of a business format or an entire business system to franchisees. The franchisee is required to comply with the franchisor's guidelines governing the operation, appearance, and location of the business. The quality of the products or services provided by the franchisees is typically controlled by the franchisor. The most common examples of business format franchises include restaurants, fast-food establishments, hotels, real estate agencies, convenience stores, and automobile service centers. Clearly the fastest-growing segment of franchising, business format franchises have doubled in number since 1972, when they represented 42 percent of all franchises. They account for more than 75 percent of all franchise businesses. Although these two types of franchises appear quite different on paper, the differences are sometimes blurred in practice.

§102 HISTORY AND DEVELOPMENT

Although it is considered a relatively recent development, franchising has existed in various forms since 1851. One example of the franchise concept was illustrated when Isaac Singer accepted fees from independent salesmen to acquire territorial rights to sell his recently invented sewing machines. The concept gained broader recognition with its incorporation in the marketing techniques of General Motors after 1898 and its eventual use throughout the automobile and gasoline industries by the 1930s. Elements of franchising were introduced into retail marketing with the development of the Ben Franklin general merchandise stores in 1920 and the emergence of a national network of A & W "walk-up" root beer stands after 1925. Its expansion to the emerging service sector of the economy came with the initiation of national chains of Arthur Murray Dance Studios in 1938, Baskin-Robbins ice cream stores in 1940, and Duraclean carpet cleaning services in 1943.

The decade of the 1950s was a period of significant growth and innovation in franchising. An expanding postwar economy and a growing interstate highway system encouraged the growth of gasoline stations, restaurants, and other franchise ventures directed toward an increasingly mobile U.S. public. A significant early convert to franchising was Harlan Sanders, who initiated his Kentucky Fried Chicken franchise in 1950, building a chain of more than 600 restaurants during the decade. Other franchisors, including Dairy Queen, Orange Julius, Tastee Freeze, Dunkin' Donuts, and McDonald's, followed Sanders' lead in building national chains along the growing interstate highway system.

In 1953-1954, franchising was introduced in the real estate and hotel industries. Moreover, from 1953 to 1956, franchising emerged within such diverse service industries as dry cleaning, employment services, and tax accounting. In 1950, fewer than 100 companies had employed franchising in their marketing operations. By the close of the decade, more than 900 companies had franchise operations involving an estimated 200,000 franchised outlets.

The success and rapid growth of these early franchise chains, together with an expanding economy during the mid-1960s, set off a surge of franchising activity after 1964 as hundreds of companies turned to franchising to build national marketing networks. An estimated 100,000 new franchise businesses were initiated between 1964 and 1969. Although new franchising activity began to moderate after 1979, an additional 50,000 franchises were initiated between 1969 and mid-1973, when the total number of franchised businesses reached a peak of 374,782.[1]

In the rush to begin franchising during this period, numerous franchise offerings appeared that were hastily structured, ill-conceived, and poorly capitalized. Others proved to be blatantly fraudulent. The growing number of public complaints, class action lawsuits, and business failures soon had a dampening effect on new franchise development, prompting a number of states to enact regulatory restrictions on franchise sales as early as 1970.

§103 THE ECONOMICS OF A FRANCHISE

Many economic studies have examined the franchise phenomenon. Most of these focus on the franchisor's motivations: These are, basically, to establish a rapid market presence and to obtain off-balance-sheet financing and expansion and exploitation of their trademark and goodwill. Some have cynically noted that firms offer franchises when the cost of monitoring management is high.[1] Some franchisor economics were recently disclosed in *Forbes* magazine. For example, in 1993 Boston Chicken collected $5.2 million in initial franchise fees and area development fees—12 percent of sales and three times pretax income. On the other side of the coin, McDonald's showed a gain of 634 franchised outlets in 1993, but the $24 million in initial franchise fees was minuscule in relation to its $1.1 billion in net profits.[2]

The negatives to the franchisor are related to the interdependence between the franchisor and franchisee, which can leave both parties in a somewhat precarious position. The franchisor relies on the franchisees maintaining a certain level of quality and good service. If the franchisee fails to maintain such a level, the value of the trademark declines and with it the value of the franchisor.

From the franchisee's point of view, franchise firms and nonfranchise opportunities have many similarities. However, identifying the differences allows for the creation of a theoretical valuation model to develop a franchising pricing model.

Some of the benefits that have been frequently cited are the lower rates of bankruptcy and business failures. The Small Business Administration has reported that 23.7 percent of small businesses fail within the first two years and 62.7 percent (almost two-thirds) fail within six years.[3] Prior statistics have shown that only 3.2 percent of business format franchises were discontinued in 1986.[4] However, in a recent study of nearly 1,300 franchises started between 1984 and 1987, only 55

§102 [1]Report of House Committee on Small Business, Franchising in the U.S. Economy: Prospects and Problems (U.S. Department of Commerce, Aug. 13, 1990), at 5-8.

§103 [1]Osteryoung, Hodges, & Wells, A Valuation Model for Franchise Contracts, Business Valuation Review, June 1993, p.61.

[2]Hardy, Franchise Primer, Forbes, Aug. 15, 1994, p.141.

[3]The 1989 State of Small Business: A Report of the President, at 25 (U.S. Government Printing Office).

[4]Franchising in the Economy 1986-1988, at 11 (U.S. Department of Commerce).

percent were still operating in 1991, but 73 percent of the nonretail franchises were still operating in such fields as finance, insurance, and real estate.[5]

In 1984, the U.S. Department of Commerce listed eight primary benefits accruing to a purchasing franchisee:

(1) gains from the franchisor's know-how;
(2) sharing the franchisor's success story;
(3) continuous guidance;
(4) being equipped with sales tools and administrative procedures that have been proven for maximum results;
(5) training in administrative procedures—ensuring the most effective work flow and controls;
(6) schooling and follow-up training;
(7) benefits of cooperative advertising; and
(8) advantages in site selection, lease negotiations, store layout, and other areas.

One explanation given for the better results achieved by franchises is that most franchisees are required to make some minimum equity investment. Accordingly, this suggests that most franchises will be starting out with a stronger financial base than nonfranchise operations.

A second difference is the investor's expectation of return. The incentive to purchase a franchise is that, from a cash flow point of view, the investor expects the return to exceed the return from a nonfranchise operation by more than the additional costs (i.e., franchise fee and operating royalty). Basically, the economic literature holds that the value of a franchise is the present value of the difference in cash flows generated by a nonfranchise and a franchise firm. Attorneys and accountants should not consider this too esoteric a field because it should also play a large part in any damages computation involving franchise litigation or in the area of estate and succession planning as discussed below.

§104 FRANCHISING IN THE 1990s

Franchising emerged as a significant force in the nation's economy during the 1980s and 1990s. Franchising showed steady and impressive growth throughout the decade in both franchise sales and the growth of new franchise businesses. Despite severe recessionary conditions during 1982-1983, the number of business format franchises increased by nearly 51,000 between 1980 and 1986.[1]

Sales of products and services by all franchises grew by $198 billion, or 69 percent, during the six years between 1980 and 1986. Combined sales grew annually at an impressive rate of 9 percent during the recession years prior to 1983

[5]Wall St. J., Feb. 28, 1995, at B2 (citing a study by economist Timothy Bates). Some franchisors and their allies raise questions about Dr. Bates' methodology.

§104 [1]The year 1986 was the last complete year for which the Commerce Department compiled data on franchise sales and growth.

and then accelerated to nearly 11 percent between 1983 and 1986. Business format franchises continued to register particularly high levels of annual increases in sales, averaging 10 percent during 1980-1983 and 14.5 percent as economic conditions improved after 1983.

A variety of economic, demographic, and social factors influenced the growth of both the service sector and the franchising industry during the 1980s and 1990s. The aging of the huge baby-boom generation, the surge of women entering the work force, the growing number of active retirees, and the emergence of two-income families helped create tremendous demand for services ranging from day care and house cleaning to drive-through fast food and auto maintenance. Businesses also created new demands for services seeking to cut operating costs by contracting for everything from janitorial services to personnel and accounting services. Changing attitudes regarding convenience, product quality, emerging technologies, mass advertising, and other factors further encouraged development of a wide variety of service-oriented business opportunities.

A rising sense of entrepreneurism among key groups within the population, together with increasing limits on the ability of companies to expand by more traditional means, provided a growing pool of potential franchisees and franchisors willing to undertake new ventures in response to these business opportunities. Furthermore, the enormous corporate downsizing that has progressed through the 1980s and 1990s has resulted in the layoff of an enormous number of middle managers who have accumulated some financial substance and have become a vast new pool of potential franchisees.

Faced with intense competition for increasingly scarce top-level corporate jobs, members of the huge baby-boom generation have sought out entrepreneurial opportunities in increasing numbers as a means of gaining more enjoyment, less structure, or greater control over their working schedules. The narrowing economic opportunities have also prompted an increasing number of women, minorities, early retirees, and immigrants to seek out franchising and other business opportunities.

At the same time, existing businesses have sought alternative, less costly methods for expanding operations and distribution networks in response to rising capital costs, unfavorable tax changes, and growing pressure to reduce costs and eliminate debt. Franchising has provided the means for merging the seemingly conflicting interests of existing businesses with those of aspiring entrepreneurs in a single process that promotes business expansion, entrepreneurial opportunity, and shared cost and risk.

Prompted by these influences, the pace of franchising activities has accelerated since the mid-1980s. The number of companies initiating franchise programs almost doubled during the decade, increasing gradually from approximately 1,600 in 1980 to 2,100 at the end of 1985, then exploding to an estimated 3,000 in 1989. Commerce Department projections of franchise growth also show an accelerating pace in the development of new franchises, estimating the addition of 50,000 new business format franchises during 1987-1988, nearly double the number added during 1985-1986.

The Commerce Department's estimate of 416,878 franchise business operations in 1988 represented a net increase of 61,000 (17 percent) over the number in operation in 1980. This figure includes the addition of approximately 100,000 new business format franchises initiated during 1980-1988 (an increase of 52 percent), offset by the loss of an additional 40,000 product/trade name franchises. The estimated 27,273 new franchise units opened during 1988 represented the addition of one franchise every 20 minutes throughout the year.

The 416,878 franchise businesses operating in 1988 employed an estimated 7 million workers and had estimated sales of $543 billion. Sales by business format franchises were estimated to have increased by 12 percent annually during 1987-1988, with a slower 4 percent growth in sales among product/trade name franchises. The estimated $543 billion in combined sales by all franchise businesses in 1988 represented an increase of 90 percent over annual franchise sales in 1980 and accounted for approximately one-third of all U.S. retail sales.[2]

In 1995, according to the International Franchise Association, more than 550,000 franchise businesses dot the American landscape, generating more than $800 billion in sales. And the growth has become even more rapid than during the 1980s, with a new franchise business opening somewhere in the United States every eight minutes each business day.

Business format franchises (excluding gasoline and bottling franchises) showed substantial growth in the number of outlets: 353,000 in 1989, 386,000 in 1990, 408,000 in 1991, and 428,000 in 1992. The sales of these business format franchises also showed remarkable growth: $193 billion in 1989, $213 billion in 1990, $232 billion in 1991, and $248 billion in 1992.

§105 INTERNATIONAL FRANCHISING

A major development in franchising during the past decade has been the expansion of U.S. franchise businesses throughout the world. From Western Europe to South Asia and Australia, franchise companies have found receptive markets and significant opportunities to expand sales of products and services or to export their methods of operation. Recently, enormous growth has been found in the former Communist countries of Eastern Europe and in Japan, Mexico, and many other South American countries. Unlike companies seeking only to market U.S. products or establish U.S.-owned facilities, franchises offer opportunities for local ownership within a foreign market while providing U.S. business methods, knowledge, and technology. This has made franchising particularly attractive in many parts of the world, with U.S. franchisors often finding themselves in the role of recruiters rather than salesmen.

Approximately 260 U.S. companies operated 17,000 franchise outlets outside the United States in the late 1970s. By 1986, the last year for which Commerce Department figures are available, the number of franchisors with foreign operations had increased to 354, with total outlets approaching 32,000. The Commerce

[2]Report of House Committee on Small Business, Franchising in the U.S. Economy: Prospects and Problems (Aug. 13, 1990), at 11-14.

Department's figures also indicated an additional 288 franchise companies with plans to expand abroad before 1990.[1]

Canada has provided the most popular foreign market for expansion by U.S. franchisors. As the nation's largest trading partner, Canada has proven extremely receptive to U.S. franchisors and has imposed few legal or regulatory restrictions on franchise operations. An estimated 240 U.S. companies operated 9,031 franchises in Canada in 1986, representing 29 percent of all U.S. franchises abroad. Canada has also developed a growing franchising sector of its own with some 1,200 Canadian and U.S. companies operating Canada-based franchise businesses with more than 60,000 outlets and annual sales of $67 billion. Franchising constitutes the fastest growing method of business expansion in Canada.

England, Australia, and other British Commonwealth countries have also provided active and growing markets for U.S. franchises. American franchises, particularly restaurant and fast-food outlets, began to appear in England and Australia in the late 1960s. Franchising now accounts for more than 11 percent of annual retail sales in England. Australia ranked third in 1986 (behind Canada and Japan) in the number of operating U.S. franchises with 2,816, followed by England with 2,415.

Japan has also offered a large and lucrative market for those U.S. franchisors that have been able to establish operations there. In 1987, nearly 70 U.S. companies operated a total of 7,366 franchise units in Japan. Entry into the Japanese market has proved extremely difficult and costly, with negotiations often extending for 10 years or more.

Continental Europe also offers an attractive and increasingly important market for U.S. franchise operations. American franchisors are seeking to structure subfranchise arrangements within Europe in anticipation of *new barriers* to non-European firms and products after 1993. Facilitating introduction of new franchise networks within the European Community is the adoption by the European Economic Commission (EEC) of a "block exemption" for franchising that permits, among other things, a single trademark application under uniform EEC regulations instead of separate national registration requirements.

International franchising has also become a two-way process, with an increasing number of foreign companies seeking franchise opportunities in the United States. Patterns of foreign-affiliated franchise development have closely paralleled U.S. franchise activities abroad, with Canadian, British, and Japanese firms accounting for a large portion of all foreign-sponsored franchises. Canadian companies have the largest presence in the U.S. market and have generally followed the pattern in the United States of building franchise chains by opening one unit at a time.

The internationalization of U.S. franchising presents U.S. franchisors with enormous opportunities. Although this may represent franchising's ultimate triumph, it may bring increasing scrutiny of the issues and problems that have plagued franchising's development since the 1950s. Companies establishing franchises abroad have sought to apply U.S. franchise agreements to foreign franchisees and extend coverage of U.S. laws to resolve disputes arising under these agreements.

§105 [1]Survey data from Report of House Committee on Small Business, Franchising in the U.S. Economy: Prospects and Problems (U.S. Department of Commerce, Aug. 13, 1990), at 7-10.

While this is clearly beneficial to franchisors, it is likely to give rise to growing complaints abroad regarding the excessive detail and restrictions of U.S. contracts and perceived inadequacies in U.S. laws and regulations.[2]

§106 REGULATION OF FRANCHISE SALES AND DISCLOSURE

There is no federal law governing franchising relationships or practices. In addition, federal franchise disclosure requirements have been weakly enforced. State franchise laws, applicable to only one-third of all franchises, impose requirements and procedures that are inconsistent with one another and with federal requirements. This confusing regulatory environment has frustrated franchisors and fostered continuing problems and complaints among potential investors and franchisees.

Legislative and regulatory effort tend to reflect the concerns of franchisees, or potential franchisees, which fall generally within two broad groups. The first group involves problems that arise prior to entering into a franchise relationship, namely, deception or impropriety in the presentation, solicitation, or sale of a franchise opportunity. The second group involves problems arising within ongoing franchising relationships, generally involving contract performance, termination, or renewal of franchise agreements.

In attempting to redress the informational imbalance between franchisors and franchisees, the Federal Trade Commission (FTC) and various state governments have adopted regulatory procedures involving presale disclosure of material facts of a franchise offering, with penalties for false or incomplete information. This approach was first adopted in the California Franchise Investment Act of 1970, which had its roots in earlier unsuccessful efforts by the state to classify franchise opportunities as investment securities and to apply existing disclosure and registration requirements under state securities laws. The presale disclosure procedures of the California law influenced the adoption of similar requirements by 13 states between 1971 and 1980 and provided the model for the FTC's franchise disclosure rule.

§106.1 The FTC Franchise Disclosure Rule

Federal authority to regulate franchise sales derives from the FTC's Trade Rule 436, Disclosure Requirements and Prohibitions Concerning Franchising and Business Opportunities Ventures.[1] This rule is intended to provide prospective franchisees with the information necessary to make informed decisions by requiring franchisors or franchise brokers to disclose detailed information relating to 20 separate aspects of a franchise offering. Information to be disclosed includes

[2]Id. at 16-20.

§106 [1]16 C.F.R. ch. 1, pt. 436, 43 Fed. Reg. 59,614. (Dec. 21, 1978).

all relevant facts about the identity, location, business experience, and financial background of the franchisor. Detailed descriptions of the franchise opportunity, including all initial and continuing fees and payments, as well as an explanation of all terms, obligations, conditions, and requirements of the franchise agreement, should also be disclosed.

Under the rule, franchisors are not required to make claims regarding actual or potential sales, income, or profits of existing or proposed franchises. If a franchisor chooses to make such claims, however, the rule prescribes the manner of filing claims and lists the requirements necessary to establish a reasonable basis to substantiate the accuracy of all claims filed. Failure to provide the information required under the rule, providing false information, or providing information inconsistent with that required under the rule is considered a violation of the Franchise Investment Act and is subject to civil penalty actions with fines up to $10,000 per violation.

To simplify disclosure and encourage compliance with both federal and state disclosure requirements, the FTC permitted franchisors to use either the disclosure format provided in its franchise rule or a similar set of detailed guidelines incorporated in the Uniform Franchise Offering Circular (UFOC). The UFOC had been developed by the Midwest Securities Commissioners Association in 1975 to eliminate confusion and assist compliance by national franchisors that were confused by the growing number of divergent state disclosure requirements. Based on the detailed disclosure criteria of the 1970 California franchise statute, the UFOC requires information under 23 parts, or "items," that closely approximate those of the FTC rule. Although acknowledging differences between the two sets of guidelines, the FTC determined that use of the UFOC, and any minor modifications made by states that do not diminish its requirements, would provide protection to prospective franchisees "which is equal to or greater than that provided by the [Federal] rule."[2] With the advantage of prior use and detailed instructions, the UFOC became the disclosure format used almost universally by franchisors.

Franchise disclosure documents, or "circulars," prepared by franchisors under UFOC are subject to review and enforcement by both the FTC and state agencies. In general, the FTC presumes the adequacy and accuracy of circulars submitted under state registration procedures, while reserving authority to determine compliance in nonregulation states and to enforce its rule against broad violations by national franchisors.

§106.2 *State Regulatory Activity*

Most states regulate some aspect of franchise sales or relationships under a variety of business opportunity, unfair trade practices and industry regulation statutes. All states, for example, have enacted some form of a "little FTC Act," prohibiting unfair methods and deceptive acts in trade or commerce. Nearly three-quarters of the states have business opportunity statutes prohibiting fraud and

[2]Final Franchise Rule, 43 Fed. Reg. 59,752 (Dec. 21, 1978).

misrepresentation in the sale of franchises and other business opportunities. Most states have industry relationship laws regulating automobile dealerships, gasoline franchises, farm equipment dealers, or alcoholic beverage distributorships. In fact, 17 states have adopted laws governing some aspect of the substantive relationship between franchisors and franchisees.

The states generally considered to be regulating states in the franchising industry are the 15 states that have enacted statutes specifically regulating franchise solicitations and sales. These states account for one-third of the nation's population, more than one-third of all franchises, and the overwhelming majority of all franchise enforcement actions. Thirteen of these states—California, Hawaii, Illinois, Indiana, Maryland, Minnesota, New York, North Dakota, Rhode Island, South Dakota, Virginia, Washington, and Wisconsin—require both presale disclosure and registration of disclosure documents with state agencies. Of the two remaining states, Oregon has enacted specific franchise disclosure requirements without requiring a registration process, whereas Michigan requires disclosure but dropped registration procedures in 1984.

The 13 states with franchise disclosure and registration procedures operate under statutes that are relatively uniform. They require comprehensive presale disclosures to prospective franchisees using the UFOC guidelines. These statutes also impose similar procedures for state agency review and approval of franchise circulars prior to certifying a franchise sale. State agencies may require changes in a circular, request additional information or documentation, or refuse to register the franchise offering. All 13 statutes provide civil and criminal sanctions for violations; most provide remedial rights for individuals injured by such violations.

Whereas the state statutes have significant similarities in requirements and procedures, many impose additional requirements or specific language not incorporated in standard UFOC guidelines.

In addition, 19 states have enacted laws that seek to protect franchisees from arbitrary termination or nonrenewal. These states include Arkansas, California, Connecticut, Delaware, Hawaii, Illinois, Indiana, Kentucky, Louisiana, Michigan, Minnesota, Mississippi, Missouri, Nebraska, New Jersey, South Dakota, Virginia, Washington, and Wisconsin.

These variations among state laws and procedures confront franchising companies with a confusing patchwork of regulatory requirements that can make compliance not only burdensome but also potentially hazardous. Technical noncompliance with a state franchise registration law, even if due to inadvertent or honest mistakes, can taint a franchise program or, at the least, delay or discourage franchise sales. The process of compliance is difficult even for established national franchise firms, which must either constantly revise disclosure documents or maintain stocks of many different disclosure documents. Given the differing applicability standards of state laws, a single franchise sale can require preparation of two or three different sets of state disclosure documents depending on the location of the franchisor, the franchisee, and the proposed franchise.[3]

[3]Report of House Committee on Small Business, Franchising in the U.S. Economy: Prospects and Problems (U.S. Department of Commerce, Aug. 13, 1990), at 21-29.

§107 FRANCHISE COMPANY MERGERS AND ACQUISITIONS

The detailed tax aspects of mergers and acquisitions are beyond the scope of this volume.[1] However, tax practitioners should be aware of certain franchise law issues accompanying mergers and acquisitions that, in some cases, may be more material than the tax-planning aspects of franchise law.

Many franchise agreements provide territorial exclusives to franchisees. These may be defined in terms of square miles, population densities, areas served by certain periodicals, or, in some instances, areas denominated by certain conventions in the advertising community such as major markets or ADIs (areas of dominant interest) for radio or television penetration.

When parties are anticipating the merger of two or more franchise operations, they must be careful to inspect territorial overlaps to be sure that the contemplated merger or acquisition does not work a violation of either of the potential merger partners' covenants with respect to territories. In some situations this hurdle alone may be insurmountable and may dictate against the proposed merger or acquisition.

Frequently, franchise law factors dictate that franchisees be given certain rights of rescission in the event of a merger or acquisition. This is not the norm in the combination of most distributorship entities. Therefore, this potential cost (i.e., buying back all or some of the operations pursuant to a systemwide rescission offer) must be carefully analyzed before any specific type of reorganization is analyzed under the Code to determine its tax consequences.

Antitrust issues must also be high on the list of considerations. Although antitrust law is on the checklist of items to consider in all reorganizations, it must be particularly high on the list of risks associated with a franchise company merger or acquisition.

Finally, franchise company combinations are material events for purposes of franchise filing and registration statutes. Such material events frequently require separate filings and amendments to the basic franchise documents. More important, in many instances there are severe restrictions against the franchisor's selling any franchises or soliciting any new franchisees during the amending process brought on by the proposed merger or acquisition. These and all other franchise law components of such a proposed transaction must be carefully reviewed along with the determination of whether it should be structured as a "B" or "C" reorganization.[2]

§107 [1]For a detailed discussion of mergers and acquisitions, see Ginsburg & Levin, Mergers, Acquisitions and Buyouts: Transactional Analysis (The Little, Brown Tax Practice Series Jan. 1995).

[2]See Code §368(a)(1)(B) and (C).

2

Overview of Structuring Options for Franchise Relationships

§201 Franchise Arrangements, Generally
§202 Initial Franchise Fees
  §202.1 Intangibles (Including Protection Radius)
  §202.2 Site Selection and Approval
§203 Royalties, License Fees, or Service Fees
§204 Additional Services
§205 Transfer Fees
§206 Master Licensees
  §206.1 Territorial Agreements
  §206.2 Development Schedules
§207 Advertising Funds

§201 FRANCHISE ARRANGEMENTS, GENERALLY

Most modern-day franchises, particularly business format franchises, involve not only a transfer of a franchise, trademark, or trade name incident to the transfer of the business but also the agreement to provide substantial services to franchise owners. Business format franchising is characterized by ongoing business relationships between the franchisor and franchisees. This relationship typically includes the product or service, trademarks, and trade names, as well as the entire business concept—operating manuals and standards, quality control, marketing strategies and plans, and a continuing process of guidance and assistance to franchisees. Many of these franchise arrangements require the payment of an initial franchise fee upfront, ongoing royalty, license or service fees, assessments for pooled advertising funds, and specific additional charges for optional services to be rendered to the franchisee.

Prior to the Tax Reform Act of 1969,[1] tax treatment of payments for franchising operations was not specifically addressed by the Internal Revenue Code. Prior to the 1969 legislation, parties to a franchise agreement were able to characterize the

§201 [1]Pub. L. No. 91-172, 91st Cong., 1st Sess. (1969 Act).

transaction for tax purposes as they saw fit. This led to inconsistent positions taken by both franchisors and franchisees, many times resulting in the parties taking conflicting positions on the same transaction. So much confusion and contradiction encompassed early court decisions that there were even conflicting conclusions on similar arrangements among the circuit courts. In light of the diverse decisions found among the circuits regarding the tax treatment of franchise fees, Congress addressed these issues in the 1969 legislation by adding Code §1253, Transfers of Franchise, Trademarks, and Trade Names. Congress sought in the new legislation to completely address the tax treatment of franchise payments as well as payments received for trademarks and trade names. Since the enactment of Code §1253, there have been relatively few court decisions in this area. A more thorough discussion of the legislative history behind Code §1253 can be found in Chapter 3.

Code §1253(a) provides that a transfer of a franchise, trademark, or trade name is not a sale or exchange of a capital asset if the franchisor retains significant powers, rights, or a continuing interest with respect to the franchise. Unless the transferor relinquishes all these elements, gain on the transfer must be recognized as ordinary income. Because giving up all significant control of the franchise would defeat the purpose of many franchise relationships, tax treatment to most franchisors on such transfer payments falls within this definition, and the payments must be recognized as ordinary income.

Tax problems confronting franchisees center on the questions whether and/or when deductible payments are made to the franchisor. Tax treatment of these payments depends on the nature of the payments to the franchisor. Amounts paid to franchisors that are contingent upon the productivity, use, or disposition of the franchise are deductible as ordinary and necessary business expenses under Code §162(a) when they are paid or accrued, regardless of whether the transaction is treated as a sale or exchange of a capital asset or whether it is a mere licensing arrangement.[2] These contingent payments are in the nature of what are commonly referred to as royalties, license fees, or service fees. In many typical modern-day franchising arrangements, these contingent payments are usually assessed to compensate the franchisor for the intangible rights transferred.

Noncontingent payments made to franchisors are generally made for initial franchise transfer fees. Tax treatment of these franchisee payments is more difficult to ascertain. If the franchise transfer is treated as a sale or exchange, noncontingent payments must be capitalized whether they are down payments or installment payments made to discharge any portion of the initial franchise fee assessed to the franchisee.[3] If the franchise has a limited useful life that can be estimated with reasonable accuracy, the capitalized amount of the initial transfer fees can be depreciated.[4] However, the burden of proof of the determinable life of a franchise rests upon the franchisee. If the franchise can be renewed at the franchisee's sole option or if it is renewable indefinitely, depreciation cannot be allowed.[5]

[2]Code §1253(d)(1).
[3]Prop. Reg. §1.1253-1(c)(2).
[4]Code §1253(d)(2).
[5]Stromstred v. Commissioner, 53 T.C. 330 (1969).

If noncontingent payments for a franchise transfer are treated as other than a sale or exchange under Code §1253(a), it must be determined whether the payments are lump-sum payments or periodic payments. Lump-sum payments made in discharge of a principal sum are deducted ratably over the lesser of the period of the franchise agreement or 10 years.[6] Periodic payments of equal amounts made in discharge of the principal sum paid over the period of the transfer agreement, or more than 10 years, are deductible in the year paid.[7] Of course, there are many other possible payment arrangements that fall within the parameters of Code §1253. A more detailed discussion of the deductibility of payments made by franchisees can also be found in Chapter 3, "Franchise Transfers and Retransfers."

§202 INITIAL FRANCHISE FEES

Now that the background regarding the general rules for tax treatment of payments made under a franchise agreement has been elucidated, we will discuss the nature of various payments made under such arrangements and resulting structuring options to be considered for franchise relationships. Most franchisors require the payment of an initial franchise fee. Many typical modern-day franchises (particularly those of a national franchise nature) involve the transfer of intangible assets and rights, as well as the agreement to provide a substantial amount of services. Franchisees may benefit from an allocation of the initial transfer fees to specific services to be provided because payments for many of these services rendered by a franchisor may be currently deductible or depreciable over a shorter period than that authorized by Code §1253 and the accompanying proposed regulations. If one arrives at the allocation of the initial franchise fee in an arm's-length negotiation between the franchisor and the franchisee and negotiations are properly documented in an agreement entered into by the parties to the contract, the proposed regulations make it clear that the allocations set forth in the agreement will be given weight provided they are reasonable. Although the IRS is not bound by the agreement, the courts are not likely to overrule and change the terms of the contract. Although this position has not been tested in the courts, franchisees have a reasonable basis for taking this position when the franchisor is required to perform specific services for the franchisee under the terms of the agreement.

§202.1 *Intangibles (Including Protection Radius)*

Proposed income tax regulations stipulate that when fees are received for a transfer of a franchise, they must be allocated between the tangible assets and the intangible assets associated with the transfer.[1] The amount attributable to the transfer of the franchise, trademark, or trade name is to be determined on the basis of the facts and circumstances involved in each case, including any written

[6]Code §1253(d)(2)(A).
[7]Prop. Reg. §1.1253-1(c)(3)(ii).
§202 [1]Prop. Reg. §1.1253-1(d)(1).

agreements entered into by the parties to the contract.[2] However, to the extent the circumstances do not show otherwise, that portion of the amount attributable to the transfer of a trade or business that is not attributable to the transfer of specific tangible assets is to be treated as being attributable to the transfer of intangible assets.[3] Of course, a portion of most initial franchise fees is specifically used for the transfer of the intangible assets involved, including the trademarks, trade names, and business systems.

Oftentimes, franchise agreements provide for a nonrefundable portion of the initial franchise transfer fee. This portion of the fee is frequently tied to exclusive access to a defined geographic area should the other terms of the agreement be met and the new franchise location be opened. Such a nonrefundable or otherwise allocable portion of the initial franchise fee should be treated under the general rules for deductibility of franchise fees allocated to the intangible assets. In the case of franchise agreements with a perpetual nature, this portion of the fee should be depreciated over a 10-year term. Many franchise agreements, particularly those involving business format franchises, will provide for some type of protection radius from the franchised location.

§202.2 *Site Selection and Approval*

As mentioned previously, franchisors typically provide assistance to franchisees for these initial transfer payments. Among the services generally performed before the franchise location opens are the selection of an appropriate location for establishing the new franchise trade or business (or, at least, a requirement for a site approval); lease negotiations, either with outsiders or with the franchisor itself if the company owns and leases the real estate; equipment and other fixed asset planning; and planning of the proper layout and design for the location selected. Many other services are provided either at the time the franchise location opens or shortly thereafter, including initial home-office training of the franchise owners or their designees, training of new employees at the business, and on-site training and supervision of the new proprietors and other management personnel. Much assistance is also provided in the areas of marketing and advertising of the franchise, including development of marketing programs, design of the initial advertising campaigns, production of generic television, radio and print media advertisements, and planning for the grand opening of the new location.

§203 ROYALTIES, LICENSE FEES, OR SERVICE FEES

After a franchise is opened and operating, there is often a requirement in the agreement for the payment of royalties, license fees, or service fees. These fees might or might not be tied to specific services to be performed by the franchisor. These ongoing payments are most often contingent in nature, based on a percent-

[2]Id.
[3]Id.

age of sales at the franchise location. However, franchise arrangements can call for ongoing fixed payments. In either case, there are reporting requirements to be met by the franchisee so that the franchisor can monitor the success of the location. For consistency, the franchisor often controls this reporting with the use of standardized reporting forms. In addition, some ongoing payment arrangements for contingent fees provide for a sliding scale that will allow the franchisee to reduce the level of the contingent payments after ascertaining certain sales volumes.

§204 ADDITIONAL SERVICES

Due to the competitive nature of the franchise industry, many franchisors also offer additional optional services to their franchisees, which can generate additional income for the franchisor. Some examples of the additional services made available are bookkeeping and check-writing services, national reservation services, toll-free national sales or information numbers, franchisee insurance or retirement administration programs, and product sales directly from the franchisor or systemwide bulk-buying programs from third-party vendors.

§205 TRANSFER FEES

In addition to the initial franchise fee, many franchisors assess a transfer fee at such time as the franchise is sold or otherwise transferred to another third party. Some franchise companies do, however, provide for a waiver of the transfer fee if the franchise is transferred to an entity controlled by the original franchisee. Whether or not a transfer fee is assessed on such transactions, the franchisor nearly always maintains the right to approve any transfer of ownership of the franchise.

§206 MASTER LICENSEES

One of the current trends in the franchise industry is multiunit franchisee ownership. Strong franchises have learned that market penetration, bulk-buying power, and significant operating efficiencies are created by ownership of multiple franchise locations. These franchisees have become much more sophisticated. It is not uncommon to find franchisees that are larger and financially stronger than the franchisor. There is an abundance of multiunit franchisees that have even completed successful public offerings.

§206.1 *Territorial Agreements*

Based in part on the current trend of multiunit franchise owners, some franchisors are now granting exclusive territorial franchises to develop their franchise systems more rapidly. In fact, these territorial agreements are now often the sole means of developing certain franchise systems. Under such an arrangement, the franchisor may allow the territorial licensee to expand by building additional company-owned franchisee locations or to subfranchise within the territory. Generally, under such an arrangement, the franchisor will share the initial franchise fees and ongoing royalties, license fees, or service fees with the subfranchisor. Of course, the subfranchisor will most likely be required to perform many of the services required of the franchisor under the standard franchise agreement.

§206.2 *Development Schedules*

Regardless of how the expansion occurs under the territorial arrangements, there will nearly always be a certain defined development schedule tied to the agreement whereby the area developer is required to have opened additional company-owned outlets or subfranchised outlets within various time intervals. If the development schedule is not met, the area developer's rights are forfeited and the territory can be resold to another party. These territorial agreements often are referred to as area development agreements and / or master license agreements. This franchise structuring option is common for international expansion, where there are cultural, language, and other business barriers requiring a local partner or other local presence.

As with the area development or master license agreements, most franchises are granted for a specific term. Although some franchise agreements are renewable at the franchisee's option, many franchisors require the franchisee to go through a complete rewrite exercise (including execution of the current franchise agreement) upon expiration of the term of the original agreement. This gives the franchisor the opportunity to remove problem franchisees from the system. It also strengthens the potential filing position for new third-party franchisees for the amortization of intangible franchise rights over the remaining term of the existing franchise agreement after purchasing from the original franchisee. This position has been argued by taxpayers for many years, and the IRS has now issued a favorable ruling on this matter.[1]

In order to maintain quality control and other standards, the franchise agreement should contain certain provisions regarding termination for good cause. Of course, the agreement can outline many specific consequences to the franchisee as a result of the termination, including damages or other remuneration payable to the franchisor. Most franchise agreements will require some type of franchisee reporting requirements to the franchisor, particularly when the arrangement requires an ongoing contingent royalty, license fee, or service fee based on a percentage of franchisee sales. These agreements can require the franchisee to complete the reporting in a specific format or even on preprinted reporting forms provided by the franchisor. In addition, the agreement can provide for random auditing of the reports by franchisor personnel of outside parties verifying the accuracy of

§206 [1]Rev. Rul. 88-24, 1988-1 C.B. 306.

the franchisee's reports and contingent payments. Under many state statutes, however, the franchisor must provide the franchisee with written notice within a prescribed time prior to the date the company intends to exercise its verification powers.

§207 ADVERTISING FUNDS

Most franchisors provide for the establishment of pooled advertising funds. These funds create advertising programs designed to build sales for the franchisee locations and to promote the chain's identity. They also allow the franchisor to produce advertising materials for individual franchisees and to pool resources for more cost-effective radio, television, and print media advertising. Many nationally pooled franchisee advertising funds are established by the franchisor and, like the royalties, license fees, or service fees, are based on a percentage of sales. However, the assessments to the franchisees can be a flat amount of an assessment based on a proration of the actual costs incurred. The franchisor can administer the national advertising fund or it can be administered by a representative group of franchisees. An alternative approach to such advertising funds is to provide for the organization of advertising cooperatives, which are administered locally to achieve the same basic objectives. Another option is for the franchisor not to get involved in any such advertising fund administration but rather to require a minimum level of expenditures for advertising purposes by each franchisee. A final option would be to use any combination of the above structured advertising techniques.

Each franchisor has several options for franchise arrangement relationships. These arrangements can differ substantially from one franchise to another, based on a number of factors including the nature of the business, the needs for capital, the amount of services to be provided to franchisees, the type of franchising considered most appropriate, and the need for structured systemwide advertising. The franchisor can make a profit in a number of ways. For example, the franchisor can charge a substantial initial franchise fee and/or master license fee and a minimal (or no) ongoing royalty, license fee, or services fee. Alternatively, the franchisor can charge a relatively small initial franchise fee up front and assess significant ongoing license fees and advertising assessments over which it has total discretion. The franchisor can also profit substantially from performing other services for franchisees. The possibilities are countless.

3

Franchise Transfers and Retransfers

§301 Franchise Transfers, Generally
§302 Legislative History
§303 Characterization and Recognition of Receipts by the Franchisor
  §303.1 Initial Franchise Fees
  §303.2 Royalties, License Fees, or Service Fees
  §303.3 Master License Fees
  §303.4 Subsequent Transfer Fees
§304 Deductibility of Franchise Costs by Franchisees
  §304.1 Initial Franchise Fees
    §304.1.1 Prior Law
    §304.1.2 Current Law—Present Cost of Acquisitions—Amortizable Franchise Fee
  §304.2 Present Discounted Value of Right to Deduct Initial Franchise Fee
  §304.3 Master License Fees
  §304.4 Subsequent Transfer Fees
§305 Different Treatment of Franchisor and Franchisee
§306 A Modest Proposal—The Overriding Royalty
§307 Unbundling of Initial Franchise Fees
§308 Purchases of Existing Franchise Operations at a Premium: Goodwill or Franchise Rights?
§309 *Canterbury v. Commissioner*
  §309.1 Introduction
  §309.2 Goodwill and Going-Concern Value
    §309.2.1 Goodwill in the Normal Business Context
    §309.2.2 In the Normal Franchise Context
    §309.2.3 The Unique McDonald's Facts
  §309.3 The IRS Arguments in *Canterbury*
    §309.3.1 Franchisor's "Franchisee Fee" for New Franchises Establishes Amount That Can Be Amortized as "Franchise Fee"
    §309.3.2 Purchaser of Operating Franchise May Not Amortize Amount as a Franchise Fee Greater Than Amount Original Franchisee Paid

§309.3.3 Purchaser of Operating Franchise Acquires Other Nonamortizable Assets Such as Goodwill and Large Portion of Purchase Price Should Be Allocated to Those Intangibles
§310 Code §1060 Requirements Regarding Transfers and Retransfers
§310.1 Legislative History of Code §1060
§310.2 Allocation of Consideration Under the Residual Method
§310.3 Required Reporting and Compliance

§301 FRANCHISE TRANSFERS, GENERALLY

The start of a franchise operation generally involves the transfer of certain rights and know-how in exchange for payment. Most transfers of franchises, trademarks, and trade names now come within the rules of Code §§1253 and 197.

In the normal franchise situation there is a formal franchise agreement, which generally provides for the license of certain trademarks and the operational format for the running of the outlet. In exchange, the franchisee is generally obligated to make two forms of payment:

(1) a franchise fee—a lump-sum payment (sometimes referred to as an upfront payment), which is usually paid in full upon entering into the agreement; and
(2) royalty-continuing contingent payments (sometimes referred to as license fees or service fees), which are usually a percentage of the gross revenues of the franchise.

The definition of a franchise for Federal Trade Commission and local law purposes generally focuses on three elements: a trademark, a business plan, and a payment. The definition of what constitutes a franchise for tax law purposes is found in Code §1253(b)(1): "The term 'franchise' includes an agreement which gives one of the parties to the agreement the right to distribute, sell, or provide goods, services, or facilities, within a specified area."

The thrust of Code §1253 is that a transfer of a franchise shall not be treated as a sale or exchange of a capital asset if the transferor retains any significant power, right, or continuing interest. Under Code §§1253 (prior to 1993) and 197, the transferee will obtain an asset that can be amortized for tax purposes with no contest as to the useful life.

Of course, Code §1253 was adopted when capital gain characterization resulted in substantially different tax rates. Even though there is no substantial current differential in the capital gain structure because of the similarity in rates, it was once of great importance and may be again if Congress enacts a capital gains tax cut.

Under Code §1253(b)(2), the term "significant power, right, or continuing interest" includes, but is not limited to, the following rights with respect to the interest transferred:

(1) a right to disapprove any assignment of such interest, or any part thereof;
(2) a right to terminate at will;
(3) a right to prescribe the standards of quality of products used or sold, of services furnished, and of the equipment and facilities used to promote such products or services;
(4) a right to require that the transferee sell or advertise only products or services of the transferor;
(5) a right to require that the transferee purchase substantially all of his supplies and equipment from the transferor; and
(6) a right to payments contingent on the productivity, use, or disposition of the subject matter of the interest transferred, is such payments constitute a substantial element under the transfer agreement.

Furthermore, under Code §1253(b)(3) the definition of transfer includes the renewal of franchise, trademark or trade name. Thus, practically every situation that requires the preparation and delivery of a franchise prospectus gives rise to a transfer covered by Code §1253.

§302 LEGISLATIVE HISTORY

To understand the rationale behind Code §1253, which was added by the Tax Reform Act of 1969,[1] it is only necessary to look at the legislative history where the reason for the adoption of Code §1253 was given. That legislative history reads as follows:

> *General reasons for change*— Since present law does not specifically deal with the transfer of a franchise, trademark, or trade name, and since there appears to be considerable diversity of opinion among courts as to whether such a transfer constitutes a license or a sale and whether part or all of the sale constitutes the sale of a capital asset, the committee agrees with the House that Congress should clarify these problems through legislation with regard to franchises. In addition, the committee believes this should encompass trademarks and trade names and also the treatment of transferees in these cases insofar as the deductibility of payments they make to transferors is concerned.[2]

The Committee Report went on to note:

> Another aspect of this problem is the inability of the courts to agree on the proper treatment of the payments received where the transfer of a particular franchise, trademark, or trade name is considered a sale rather than a license. Amounts received

§302 [1]Pub. L. No. 91-172, 91st Cong., 2d Sess. (1969 Act).
[2]See Stand. Fed. Tax Rep. (CCH) ¶32,640.022.

> by transferors from transferees are often indeterminate and may include a lump-sum payment or a fixed amount (including installment payments over a period of time) plus payments, contingent on future sales. It also would appear that the receipt of contingent payments could be viewed as constituting a continuing economic interest in the subject matter as well as being analogous to the receipt of royalty or rental income.[3]

The major issue that had all the courts confused was the characterization of the payments received by the franchisor: Were they capital gain or were they ordinary income? Code §1253 resolves the issue in practically all instances by holding the payments to be ordinary income. In light of the 1986 Act, relegating capital gains, in large part, to the dust bin of tax history, the provision would seem of little importance. However, Code §1253 in conjunction with Code §197 also govern the timing and deductibility of the payments made by the franchisee.

The section is also notable for the determination it does not govern. Proposed Regulations §1.1253-1(b) provides:

> (b) *Transferor's treatment of contingent payments.* All amounts received or accrued by the transferor on account of the transfer of a franchise, trademark, or trade name which are contingent on the productivity, use, or disposition of the franchise, trademark, or trade name transferred are includible in gross income as ordinary income. *However, treatment of such amounts as ordinary income is not determinative as to whether such amounts will be treated as royalty income for purposes of any section of the Code specifically relating to royalties.* Such determination shall be made pursuant to such section of the Code. [Emphasis added.]

The issues that arise from the characterization of payments as royalties for other purposes of the Code will be discussed in Chapter 7.

The legislative history of the adoption of Code §197, which currently applies to franchisee amortization, was an outgrowth of the tremendous backlog of disputes between taxpayers and the IRS over whether or not assets were amortizable. Under prior law, goodwill and going-concern value were not; however, under a long line of cases, similar assets by other names frequently were amortizable. At the time of the adoption of Code §197, the IRS was faced with 6,423 outstanding audit issues representing $11.1 billion in proposed adjustments[4] relating to the amortization of intangibles issue. Therefore, Congress decided that if they could not be just (and determine actual useful lives), they would be arbitrary and mandate that all "197 intangibles" (discussed below) would be amortizable over a 15-year period.

§303 CHARACTERIZATION AND RECOGNITION OF RECEIPTS BY THE FRANCHISOR

In all but the most exceptional circumstances, Code §1253 acts to characterize both the upfront franchise fee payments and the royalties (contingent payments) paid to franchisors as ordinary income.

[3]Id.

[4]BNA Daily Tax Rep. No. 191 (Oct. 5, 1993).

The timing of income to the franchisor is determined by the franchisor's normal method of accounting. In this regard, it is worthwhile to note Statement of Financial Accounting Standards No. 45, *Accounting for Franchise Fee Revenue,* of the Financial Accounting Standards Board, which provides inter alia:

> **Individual Franchise Sales**
> 5. Franchise fee revenue from an individual franchise sale ordinarily shall be recognized, with an appropriate provision for estimated uncollectible amounts, when all material services or conditions relating to the sale have been substantially performed or satisfied by the franchisor. Substantial performance for the franchisor means that (a) the franchisor has no remaining obligation or intent—by agreement, trade practice, or law—to refund any cash received or forgive any unpaid notes or receivables; (b) substantially all of the initial services of the franchisor required by the franchise agreement have been performed; and (c) no other material conditions or obligations related to the determination of substantial performance exist. If the franchise agreement does not require the franchisor to perform initial services but a practice of voluntarily rendering services exists or is likely to exist because of business or regulatory circumstances, substantial performance shall not be assumed until either the initial services have been substantially performed or reasonable assurance exists that the services will not be performed. The commencement of operations by the franchisee shall be presumed to be the earliest point at which substantial performance has occurred, unless it can be demonstrated that substantial performance of all obligations, including services rendered voluntarily, has occurred before that time.[5]

§303.1 *Initial Franchise Fees*

Financial accounting would seem to require the franchisor to postpone the recognition of the franchise fee as income until the time the site is opened for business. However, most franchisors collect a franchise fee from a prospective franchisee upon the execution of the franchise agreement. Generally speaking, for both cash- and accrual-method taxpayers, payments received as advances are income for tax purposes in the year received, provided no restriction has been placed upon their use.

It is the policy of the IRS to tax prepaid income in the year of receipt, whether the income is derived under contracts to furnish services or is prepaid rent, royalties, or bonuses. This is true regardless of whether the period covered by the prepayment is definite or indefinite. Hence, for tax purposes, the franchise fee is generally income to the franchisor upon receipt.

In certain circumstances, with proper planning and documentation, there is a possibility that the initial franchise fees can be deferred into the subsequent tax year. Under Revenue Procedure 71-21,[6] if the initial franchise fees are received "substantially for services," the services are not performed by the end of the tax year, and the services are required to be performed by the end of the succeeding

[5]Statement of Financial Accounting Standards No. 45, Accounting for Franchise Fee Revenue.
[6]1971-2 C.B. 549.

tax year, that portion of the initial franchise fee associated with the services not yet performed can be deferred to the succeeding tax year.

In order to utilize this opportunity, it may be necessary to break out the various service components of the initial franchise fee and either change the franchise agreement or draft an addendum to the agreement requiring the franchisor to perform the specific delineated services for the franchisee by the end of the franchisor's succeeding tax year.

§303.2 *Royalties, License Fees, or Service Fees*

The characterization of the continuing payments received by the franchisor from the franchisee's operations is more fully discussed at Chapter 6. For purposes of recognition, such monies are recognized as income in accordance with the franchisor's method of accounting. The time of recognizing such income should not be different for financial accounting purposes than it is for tax purposes.

§303.3 *Master License Fees*

Fees paid for area rights or master licenses (as opposed to a fee for a single site) are generally treated for tax purposes like other upfront fees received by the franchisor. However, there is some dispute with respect to such fees for financial accounting purposes. This issue is relevant to financial accounting issues and general Securities and Exchange Commission disclosure requirements. This issue is more fully reviewed at Chapter 4.

§303.4 *Subsequent Transfer Fees*

Frequently, when a successful franchisee seeks to sell its site to a successor franchisee, the franchisor will require payment of a transfer fee. Generally, the franchisor will also require the transferee to execute the current form of the franchise agreement. Transfer fees from both a tax accounting and financial accounting point of view should be treated in the same manner as other franchise fees from an original franchisee.

§304 DEDUCTIBILITY OF FRANCHISE COSTS BY FRANCHISEES

The contingent payments made by a franchisee are deductible in accordance with the franchisee's normal accounting method under Code §1253(d)(1) which provides:

(1) CONTINGENT SERIAL PAYMENTS.—

(A) IN GENERAL.—Any amount described in subparagraph (B) which is paid or incurred during the taxable year on account of a transfer, sale, or other disposition of a franchise, trademark, or trade name shall be allowed as a deduction under section 162(a)(relating to trade or business expenses).

(B) AMOUNTS TO WHICH PARAGRAPH APPLIES.—An amount is described in this subparagraph if it—

(i) is contingent to the productivity, use, or disposition of the franchise, trademark, or trade name, and

(ii) is paid as part of a series of payments—

(I) which are payable not less frequently than annually throughout the entire term of the transfer agreement, and

(II) which are substantially equal in amount (or payable under a fixed formula).

§304.1 *Initial Franchise Fees*

§304.1.1 Prior Law

Until the addition of Code §197, as part of the Omnibus Budget Reconciliation Act of 1993 (OBRA), it was generally the case that the initial franchise fee portion of the franchisee's payment generated a deduction under former Code §1253(d)(2)(A), which read:

(i) in the case of a single payment made in discharge of such principal sum, ratably over the taxable years in the period beginning with the taxable year in which the payment is made and ending with the ninth succeeding taxable year or ending with the last taxable year beginning in the period of the transfer agreement, whichever period is shorter;

(ii) in the case of a payment which is one of a series of approximately equal payments made in discharge of such principal sum, which are payable over—

(I) the period of the transfer agreement, or

(II) a period of more than 10 taxable years, whether ending before or after the end of the period of the transfer agreement, in the taxable year in which the payment is made; and

(iii) in the case of any other payment, in the taxable year or years specified in regulations prescribed by the Secretary, consistently with the preceding provisions of this paragraph.

Then Congress changed the Code to add a provision under Code §1253(d)(2)(B) to place a $100,000 limitation on the deductibility of principal sums paid as initial franchise fees. It stated that the provision described in the discussion above would not apply if the principal sum exceeded $100,000, including all payments which were part of the same transaction (or a series of related transactions).[1] Alternatively, under former Code §1253(d)(3)(B), a taxpayer could elect to recover the amounts subject to the $100,000 limitation over 25 years. With such an election, an amount

§304 [1]Code §1253(d)(2)(B).

chargeable to capital account was allowed as a deduction ratably over the 25-year period beginning with the taxable year in which the transfer occurred.[2]

These provisions, including the formerly available election, must be considered carefully for open years and audit situations (prior to August 10, 1993, the effective date of OBRA),[3] in which there are significant initial franchise fees, as is often the case with master or territorial license agreements. It is still unclear, but it may be possible that the $100,000 limitation applies to situations involving third-party purchases of existing franchise locations at a premium. The limitation must be considered in conjunction with the more detailed aspects of these situations discussed at §308 below.

§304.1.2 Current Law—Present Cost of Acquisitions—Amortizable Franchise Fee

As previously noted, OBRA added new Internal Revenue Code §197, which relates to the amortization of goodwill and certain other intangibles. Under Code §197, a new category of asset has been created: Section 197 Intangibles. These are intangible assets acquired after the date of enactment and held in connection with the conduct of a trade or business or an activity described in §212. It excludes intangibles that were created by the taxpayer.

The definition in Code §197(d) reads as follows:

(d) SECTION 197 INTANGIBLE.—For purposes of this section-

(1) IN GENERAL.—Except as otherwise provided in this section, the term 'section 197 intangible' means—

(A) goodwill,

(B) going concern value,

(C) any of the following intangible items:

(i) workforce in place including its composition and terms and conditions (contractual or otherwise) of its employment,

(ii) business books and records, operating systems, or any other information base (including lists or other information with respect to current or prospective customer),

(iii) any patent, copyright, formula, process, design, pattern, knowhow, format, or other similar item,

(iv) any customer-based intangible,

(v) any supplier-based intangible, and

(vi) any other similar item,

(D) any license, permit, or other right granted by a governmental unit or an agency or instrumentality thereof,

(E) any covenant not to compete (or other arrangement to the extent such arrangement has substantially the same effect as a covenant not to compete) entered into in connection with an acquisition (directly or

[2] Id.

[3] There is also a retroactive election under new §197 allowing a taxpayer to have its provisions apply to acquisitions after July 25, 1991, and on or before August 10, 1993. See Temp. Reg. §1.197-1T.

indirectly) of an interest in a trade or business or substantial portion thereof, and

(F) any franchise, trademark, or trade name.

The new Code §197(f) contains certain special rules. §197(f)(4) reads as follows:

(4) TREATMENT OF FRANCHISES, ETC.—

(A) FRANCHISE.—The term "franchise" has the meaning given to such term by section 1253(b)(1).

(B) TREATMENT OF RENEWALS.—Any renewal of a franchise, trademark, or trade name (or of a license, a permit or other right referred to in subsection (d)(1)(D)) shall be treated as an acquisition. The preceding sentence shall only apply with respect to costs incurred in connection with such renewal.

(C) CERTAIN AMOUNTS NOT TAKEN INTO ACCOUNT.—any amount to which section 1253(d)(1) applies shall not be taken into account under this section.

Furthermore, Code §1253(d) has been amended by striking paragraphs (2), (3), (4), and (5) and inserting the following:

(2) OTHER PAYMENTS—Any amount paid or incurred on account of a transfer, sale or other disposition of a franchise, trademark, or trade name to which paragraph (1) does not apply shall be treated as an amount chargeable to capital account.

(3) RENEWALS, ETC.—For purposes of determining the term of a transfer agreement under this section, there shall be taken into account all renewal options (and any other period of which the parties reasonably expect the agreement to be renewed).

Under the new law, the argument over whether or not intangibles are amortizable, and if so over what term, is avoided. The law now provides a 15-year uniform capitalization period.

The economic motive for enactment of Code §197 was the issue of whether such payments can be currently deductible, amortizable, or not deductible at all.

Of course, the most valuable characterization to a purchaser is to have payment deductible in full at the time it is made. This is similar to the treatment of a cash-basis taxpayer expensing an item. The IRS is opposed to this treatment on the grounds that the asset actually has a useful life, which should be extended over many years, and that, therefore, the cost should be recaptured over such extended period of time. The worst possible event is having the asset characterized as unamortizable because, in that context, the purchaser's cost can never be recovered until a subsequent disposition. If the business or asset is not disposed of, the cost can never be recovered.

§304.2 Present Discounted Value of Right to Deduct Initial Franchise Fee

The table that follows shows the present discounted value of the after-tax cost of the initial franchise fee with respect to each $100,000 of cost in five situations: (1) the $100,000 is deductible in full when paid, (2) the $100,000 is deductible over

10 years as a franchise fee (as in former Code §1253), (3) the $100,000 is deductible over a 15-year period (as in the current Section 197), (4) the $100,000 is deductible over 25 years (as in former Code §1253 for "franchise fees" greater than $100,000), and (5) the $100,000 is all unamortizable.

	Currently deductible *(1)*	*Deductible over 10 years* *(2)*	*Deductible over 15 years* *(3)*	*Deductible over 25 years* *(4)*	*Not deductible* *(5)*
Cash outlay	100,000	100,000	100,000	100,000	100,000
Less: present discounted value of tax deduction @ 8%–34% tax rate	34,000	22,814	19,404	14,517	0
Net cost	66,000	77,186	80,596	85,483	100,000

The table addresses the many ways that a purchasing franchisee may use to recoup its cost. However, this should be understood in connection with a further complication: The purchasing franchisee's treatment of the cost of acquisition for tax purposes is substantially different from the treatment of the selling franchisor (or a reselling franchisee). (See §305 below.)

§304.3 *Master License Fees*

As a general rule, area fees or master license fees paid by a multiunit franchise operator should be treated the same as upfront or other franchise fees. From the payor's point of view, there is little difference between the financial accounting and the tax accounting rules, except that financial accounting can mandate a different amortization period.

§304.4 *Subsequent Transfer Fees*

From the franchisee's point of view, subsequent transfer fees offer no unique problems. Again, they are basically treated in the same manner as any upfront or other franchise fee.

§305 DIFFERENT TREATMENT OF FRANCHISOR AND FRANCHISEE

Code §§1253 and 197 often mandate different treatment for the two sides of the same transaction. This can be illustrated as follows:

EXAMPLE

Assume that a successful franchisor is offering a valuable unit franchise, multiple franchise, subfranchise, area franchise, or master franchise in return for an initial franchise fee of $100,000. Usually, the franchisor arranges for payment of the initial franchise fee in full upon execution of the franchise agreement. If the franchisee makes such a lump-sum franchise fee payment and the term of the franchise is 10 years or longer, the Code currently requires that the payment be amortized by the franchisee over a 15-year period. If we assume that both franchisor and franchisee are paying the current maximum federal corporate rate of 34 percent and that both are using the 8 percent discount and interest factors, the tax and economic effects on the two parties to the transaction are as follows:

Franchisor	
Current Receipts	$100,000
Less: Taxes Due	34,000
Net Receipt	$ 66,000
Franchisee	
Current Cost	$100,000
Less: present discounted value of right to deduct $6,667/year each of next 15 years	19,404
Net Cost	$ 80,596

The fact that this transaction costs the franchisee more than it benefits the franchisor reflects the "deferral" tax factor, which can be considered a double-edged sword. In this instance, because the transaction involves a deferral of a tax benefit (i.e., the deduction) rather than a tax liability (i.e., the obligation to pay taxes), the franchisee is placed in the situation of having the effective rate of its tax deductions reduced to less than 20 percent, even though it is in the 34 percent bracket.

From the franchisee's point of view, if the initial franchise fee payment were currently deductible, the current value of the tax deduction would be $34,000, thus reducing the net cost of the franchisee to $66,000. This would represent a substantial reduction in the real (i.e., after-tax) cost to the franchisee. In some instances the payment of the franchise fee in staggered installments can provide economic benefit to both the franchisor and the franchisee.[1]

§305 [1]See Schaeffer, Franchise Fee Collection: Reaping the Benefit of Franchise Tax Deductions, 4 Franchise Legal Dig. 3 (1985).

§306 A MODEST PROPOSAL—THE OVERRIDING ROYALTY

The differing treatment (discussed above) of the buyer and seller results in a mismatch so that it costs the buyer more to acquire a franchise than the seller actually receives. To provide for comparable treatment for both sides of the transaction, perhaps sellers of operating franchises should borrow a concept from the oil industry—the overriding royalty.

An overriding royalty in the mineral or oil context is a right that entitles its owner to a specific fraction of production, in kind or in value, and is not burdened with the costs of development or operation. It is different from a normal royalty in that it is created from an operating interest and its term is coextensive with that of the operating interest from which it was created.

The same could apply in the franchise context. The seller of an operating franchise instead of receiving an upfront "franchise fee" (or purchase price which is amortized by the buyer under Code §1253) could take back an overriding royalty as a percentage of gross revenues, over and above the royalties paid to the franchisor.

In terms of analyzing the buyer's financial substance, the franchisor's criteria should be exactly the same as they are currently. Proposed buyers should be required to have the same amount of funds as if they were to pay an upfront "franchise fee" or purchase price. However, if the buyer and seller are willing to work together, and the seller is willing to take a portion of the sales price over time rather than all at once, the costs to the buyer can be reduced while the amount received by the seller can be increased.

This anomaly would be achieved because the mismatch between the buyer's and the seller's tax situation would be removed. Therefore, the present value cost to the buyer could be reduced while increasing the present value received to the seller. They could split the tax benefits.

Moreover, the availability of this procedure would not be affected by Code §197's new amortization provisions because the new amortization provisions do not apply to Code §1253(d)(1), Contingent Serial Payments (i.e., royalties). The overriding royalty payments would fall within Code §1253(d)(1) as amplified by Revenue Ruling 88-24, which held that payments to the seller of an operating franchise constituted payments to be treated by the transferee under Code §1253(d)(1).

Therefore, let us go back to the table in §304.2 above. As can be seen, it cost the buyer $77,186 to net the seller a present value of $66,000 if amortized over 10 years and $85,483 if amortized over 25 years.

If the buyer's cost were paid ratably as an overriding royalty over the remaining term of the franchise agreement (which we shall assume for our purposes to be 10 years), a royalty payment of $13,637 per year deductible by the buyer at a 34 percent rate and taxable to the seller at a 34 percent rate would yield net after-tax payments of $9,000 per year. Using an interest factor of 8 percent, the present discounted after-tax value of that payment equals $60,390.73. An after-tax payment of $10,000 per year (which would require a pretax royalty of $15,151) yields a present value of only $67,100.

Because the royalties would be deductible when paid by the buyer and not taxable by the seller until received, there would no longer be a mismatch. The present cost to the buyer would be exactly the same as the present value of the receipts by the seller. Therefore, a royalty of $17,424 per year before taxes for a total of $174,240 over the 10 years (which would actually cost the buyer and yield the seller $11,500 per year after taxes) would have a present discounted value of $77,165.94.

Accordingly, in terms of present discounted after-tax costs, it is no more expensive to the buyer to pay $174,240 as a royalty over 10 years than it is to pay $100,000 up front. Simply put, the seller will receive more while the buyer's costs can remain the same or be substantially reduced if the buyer would otherwise be subject to 25-year or 15-year amortization.

Franchisors may have mixed feelings about this. On the one hand, anything that effectively enhances the prices for franchise resales naturally enhances the value of the system overall. On the other hand, some franchisors may be of the opinion that once franchisees sell their operation, they want the franchisor out of their system completely. Of course, if the franchise being sold is company owned, the franchisor should have no reservations about effectively increasing its yield. If the amortization period is 10 years, the net receipts received by the seller can be increased by 16.6 percent (i.e., from $66,000 to $77,186). To the extent that the amortization period is 25 years (as under present Code §1253 to the extent that "franchise fee" exceeds $100,000) the differential is 28.7 percent, going from $66,000 to $85,483.

To determine the percentage overriding royalty that would have to be charged to equal $100,000 of purchase price, the parties would simply work backwards from the annual sales on which the royalty is based. Therefore, if, as in *Canterbury v. Commissioner*[1] there are annual sales of $1,304,541 (the revenues of Mr. Schupack's McDonald's restaurant), an overriding royalty of less than 1.5 percent of sales would yield a royalty payment of $17,424 per year. This would cost the buyer and net the seller $11,500 per year after taxes for a present value to the seller and present discounted cost to the buyer of $77,165. Such a small additional royalty in light of the fact that it would abrogate a required upfront payment should not crimp the operations of the purchasing franchisee. Such an arrangement, being tied to gross revenues, also constitutes a built-in adjustment for inflation.

Therefore, in appropriate circumstances, the overriding royalty should be considered as an alternative. Of course, such a transaction could only be structured with the express approval of the franchisor. However, if it costs nothing, and nets a selling franchisee (or, in a case of a company-owned store, a selling franchisor) more money, the idea of an overriding royalty should not be cavalierly dismissed.

§306 [1]99 T.C. No. 12, at 5090 (1992).

§307 UNBUNDLING OF INITIAL FRANCHISE FEES

As described at length in Chapter 2, most modern-day franchises involve not only the transfer of significant powers and rights to intangible assets incident to the transfer of the business but also the agreement to provide a substantial amount of services. Many of these services can be tied directly to the initial franchise transfer fee. Franchisees can benefit from allocation of the initial franchise fees to specific services to be provided because payments for many of these services rendered by the franchisor can be currently deductible or depreciable over a shorter period than that authorized by Code §1253 or §197. Franchisors can also benefit from such an allocation because unbundling of initial franchise fees can allow them to defer the income for tax purposes or accelerate income recognition for financial purposes.

Under Revenue Procedure 71-21,[1] payments received substantially for services to be rendered can be deferred for tax purposes to the next succeeding tax year from the tax year in which the payment is received in certain situations. Revenue Procedure 71-21 specifically allows an accrual-method taxpayer who receives a payment in one tax year for services that, under an agreement, are required to be performed by the end of the next succeeding tax year to exclude such payments from taxable income in the year received. Under these circumstances, the franchisor is allowed to defer only the income from the initial franchise fees attributable to services completely performed in the tax year succeeding the year of payment. If the performance of the services under any particular franchise agreement extends beyond the succeeding tax year, the entire initial franchise fee must be reported as income in the year of receipt. In order to qualify for the tax deferral, the franchisor must not only unbundle and allocate the initial franchise fee to specific services to be performed but also substantiate with reasonable certainty which of the services were actually performed by the end of the tax year.

Such a change in policy for allocation and recognition of initial franchise fees can constitute a change in method of accounting requiring permission from the Commissioner of Internal Revenue. This change of accounting method issue can be particularly sensitive if related parties are involved. In many cases, the only way to avoid an application for change in accounting method is to demonstrate and document clearly that there has been a change in the underlying facts surrounding the situation.

In order to qualify for the tax deferral and possibly accelerated recognition of the revenue for financial reporting purposes, the franchisor must delineate the specific services to be rendered and allocate the amount of the initial franchise fees associated with the performance of the specific services required. If the allocation of the initial franchise fees is arrived at in an arm's-length negotiation between franchisor and franchisee and documentation of the negotiations is properly executed in the franchise agreement or other written contracts, the proposed regulations make it clear that any reasonable allocation arrived at in the agreement will be given serious consideration.[2] Of course, the IRS is not bound by the agreement,

§307 [1]1971-2 C.B. 549.
[2]Prop. Reg. §1.1253-1(d)(1).

but the court system is not likely to overrule the terms of a negotiated contract. Therefore, it may be prudent to make changes to the standard franchise agreement or draft an addendum to the standard agreement for use in certain specific situations in which a tax deferral opportunity can arise. See Chapter 2 for a more detailed discussion of the specific services normally rendered and potential unbundling of payments for specific services for these initial franchise transfer fees.

§308 PURCHASES OF EXISTING FRANCHISE OPERATIONS AT A PREMIUM: GOODWILL OR FRANCHISE RIGHTS?

The proper treatment for the purchase price paid by a franchisee to buy an existing outlet from its current operator rather than the franchisor is an issue that has been debated for a long time and has recently received some clarification. Frequently, a franchise is purchased for significantly more than the fair market value of the underlying assets of the business, particularly when the franchise has operated profitably over an extended period of time. Under ordinary circumstances, the purchase price of the business would be allocated to the underlying assets acquired to the extent of their fair values, and the balance of the purchase price or "premium" paid would be allocated to goodwill. However, if the business acquired is a typical modern-day franchise arrangement, under certain circumstances the premium could be allocated to the cost of franchise rights. This has particular relevance for sales prior to 1993.

At first glance this distinction does not seem significant. From a tax planning perspective, however, this classification of the premium paid could be extremely important. Amortization of assets is not tax-deductible unless the assets have a fixed and determinable value and a determinable useful life. For years prior to the adoption of Code §197, goodwill had an indefinite useful life and was not amortizable.[1] Generally, other intangible assets such as patents, copyrights, licenses, franchises, contracts, or assets having limited useful lives were amortizable. In the case of a franchise acquisition, Code §1253 specifically authorized the buyer to amortize the cost of certain franchises over the lesser of either the term of the franchise agreement or 10 years (or 25 years). Until recently, it was not absolutely clear whether "premiums" paid in the acquisition fell within this definition, but then the IRS issued a ruling constituting authority for taking such a position. In any event, franchise renewal provisions and the franchisor's rewriting experience should be analyzed and documented to account for the possibility of amortizing premiums paid over the life of the asset.

The issue of classifying a premium paid for a franchise business as the cost of the franchise rights rather than goodwill was not formally challenged before the case of *Canterbury v. Commissioner*.[2] Resolving this issue had become a matter of interpretation. The IRS issued a report on audit techniques to aid the practitioner

§308 [1]Reg. §1.167(a)-3.
[2]99 T.C. No. 12, at 5090 (1992).

in the valuation of a business interest for estate tax purposes. The report specifically stated that "where the excess earning power of a concern is attributable to an asset or business advantage which cannot be conveyed to a buyer (such as a nonassignable franchise, the personal qualifications and skill of the deceased owner or an unusual consumer demand for the company's product), no transferable or marketable goodwill exists." This position also generally followed the Tax Court decisions in *Zorniger v. Commissioner*[3] and *Akers v. Commissioner*.[4] These cases were heard in Tax Court for issues involving valuation of two General Motors franchise arrangements. The court decided that these franchise rights were nontransferable and nonassignable licenses and, thus, could be terminated by the franchisor. Consequently, it was determined that no goodwill existed under these circumstances.

In 1986, the IRS held that the cost of a purchased franchise was amortizable under Code §1253(d) if the taxpayer purchased all the assets of the franchisee's business for a fixed sum and the franchisor retained "significant powers."[5] The taxpayer did not fit neatly into the Code §1253 statutory scheme because the transaction involved three parties: (1) the franchisor; (2) the original franchisee; and (3) the taxpayer. Even though the statute was written with two-party transactions in mind, the IRS held that the taxpayer fit within the intent of the statute. Nevertheless, to bridge the statutory gap, the IRS stated that, for purposes of applying Code §1253(d), the franchisor and the original franchisee (who sold its assets to the taxpayer) together should be considered the "transferor." Two other private letter rulings also supported this position.[6] When the IRS issued Revenue Ruling 88-24, it significantly solidified this position by making it clear that Code §1253 did apply to these third-party transfers.[7] Therefore, practitioners should note that there was substantial authority for amortization of premiums paid under the rules of Code §1253.

§309 *CANTERBURY V. COMMISSIONER*

§309.1 *Introduction*

On August 17, 1992, the Tax Court, by Judge Ruwe, decided the case of *Canterbury v. Commissioner*.[1] The Canterburys (and several other taxpayers whose cases were consolidated) purchased operating McDonald's restaurants at a price that exceeded the price of the tangible assets.

The taxpayers allocated the portion of the purchase price that exceeded the value of the tangible assets to the franchise and amortized that amount pursuant to Internal Revenue Code §1253(d)(2)(A), which basically provided, during the

[3]62 T.C. 435 (1974).
[4]6 T.C. 693 (1946).
[5]Priv. Ltr. Rul. 8630002 (Jan. 27, 1986); Gen. Couns. Mem. 39,539 (Jan. 22, 1986).
[6]Priv. Ltr. Ruls. 8735082 and 8735083 (June 6, 1987).
[7]Rev. Rul. 88-24, 1988-1 C.B. 306.
§309 [1]99 T.C. No. 12, at 5090 (1992).

time at issue, for the amortization of such costs over a period of 10 years. The restaurants at issue in *Canterbury* were acquired in the years between 1972 and 1984 (this gives some idea of the length of time it takes to resolve a tax dispute with the IRS).

The Internal Revenue Service's position in *Canterbury* was that the taxpayers had allocated too much to the "franchise fee" and that such amounts should be allocated to unamortizable assets such as goodwill and going-concern value. The IRS argued at trial that the amount the taxpayers could deduct as the "franchise fee" for purposes of Code §1253 was limited to the amount the franchisor charged the original franchisee.

Judge Ruwe's decision ripped through the IRS position. The court held that with the exception of a relatively small allocation to going-concern value, the remainder of the purchase price (over the cost of the tangible assets) was properly allocable to the "franchise fee" and therefore amortizable under Code §1253.

What was at stake was whether the purchaser of a going franchise could deduct the entire intangible cost as opposed to the purchaser of a normal going business operation who was obligated to allocate a portion of such cost to nonamortizable "goodwill" and like assets: in other words, whether a business could be paid for with pretax or after-tax dollars.

The Service's position and evidence at trial were poor at best. Their arguments bordered from weak to desperate and conflicted with their own published revenue rulings.

But perhaps the franchise community should not take undue comfort from the decision. McDonald's in general and the stipulated facts in particular make for an almost unique fact pattern that purchasers of other franchises may not be able to duplicate.

§309.2 *Goodwill and Going-Concern Value*

"Goodwill" and "going-concern" value are the intangible asset characterizations that a purchaser is least likely to want to use in the acquisition of an operating business. The IRS, on the other hand, under prior law was going to argue that the taxpayer purchased goodwill and going-concern value. The reason for the IRS position was simple: Because goodwill and going-concern value were considered to have no ascertainable useful life, they were unamortizable. Thus the taxpayer had less deductions and, therefore, the Treasury more revenues.

§309.2.1 Goodwill in the Normal Business Context

As the court said in *Canterbury*:

> One of the principal intangible assets likely to be found when ownership of an operating business is transferred is goodwill. Goodwill represents the expectancy that old customers will resort to the old place of business [citation omitted]. The essence of goodwill is a pre-existing business relationship founded upon a continuous

> course of dealing that can be expected to continue indefinitely [citation omitted]. Goodwill is characterized as the expectancy of continued patronage for whatever reason [citation omitted].[2]

Another intangible often acquired when an operating business is transferred is going-concern value. Although in *Canterbury* there had been a stipulation of a minimum allocation to going-concern value nonetheless, the court addressed the issue. The court described this intangible as follows:

> Going concern value is defined as the additional element of value which attaches to property by reason of its existence as an intricate part of a going concern [citation omitted]. Going concern value relates less to the business reputation and the strength of customer loyalty than to the operating relationship of assets and personnel inherent in an on-going business [citation omitted]. Going concern value is characterized by the availability of an acquired business to continue to operate and generate income without interruption during and after acquisition [citations omitted].[3]

§309.2.2 In the Normal Franchise Context

(1) *Goodwill.* In practically every franchise agreement there are specific contract clauses dealing with goodwill. Although the specific wording may vary, the essence of every such contract clause is that all goodwill inures to the benefit of the franchisor, and that the franchisee specifically disclaims any rights in such goodwill. The McDonald's franchise agreement included the following clauses:

> In the event of such a termination [i.e. for franchisee's breach] there shall be no payment by Licensor for intangible assets of Licensee" and, more specifically:
>
> Licensee acknowledges . . . (g) That McDonald's is the sole owner of the trademarks, trade names, service marks and goodwill associated therewith, and Licensee acquires no right, title, or interest in those names and marks other than the right to use them only in the manner and to the extent prescribed and approved by Licensor.[4]

Strangely, this issue of contractually reserved goodwill was not addressed at all by the court in *Canterbury.*

(2) *Going-concern value.* A franchised business cannot be operated at all without the consent of the franchisor. The consent and license granted by the franchisor is embodied in the franchise agreement; it is characterized for tax purposes as the "franchise rights." Accordingly, an argument can easily be made that without the franchise rights the business simply would not be allowed to operate; therefore, no allocation should be given to going-concern value separate and apart from franchise rights.

However, as noted above, in the *Canterbury* case going-concern value was not really before the court. It was the subject of a separate stipulation. The court

[2] Id.
[3] Id. at 5103.
[4] Special thanks to Paul J. Schaffhausen, Federal Tax Counsel, McDonald's Corporation.

referred to an acceptance by both sides "that operating McDonald's restaurants have comparatively little going-concern value, when that term is understood to mean avoided start-up costs."[5] The court felt they should accept the determination of the taxpayer's expert that such "avoided start-up costs" constituted the amount of going-concern value that was separate from the franchise.

The essence of the franchise relationship is that the franchisee is buying the franchisor's know-how. Clearly this know-how embodies many elements closely associated with the start-up of the business. Intellectually, it is very difficult to see how these avoided start-up costs can be segregated from the general franchise rights (e.g., site selection, design, and advertising), all of which are generally provided as part of the franchise rights.

§309.2.3 The Unique McDonald's Facts

The "findings of fact" in the *Canterbury* case run almost 11 pages of double-column small type. It is as close to a court-ordered public relations piece as can be found. It is absolutely laudatory of McDonald's. The court discusses the history and philosophy of McDonald's franchising system, particularly emphasizing the philosophy of the founder, Ray Kroc, that "high upfront franchise fees could prevent franchisees from making a reasonable profit."[6] Therefore, there was a particular corporate policy to maintain low franchise fees. How many franchisors operate under the same philosophy?

The court found, "The initial franchise fee charged by McDonald's was $950.00 until 1960, $12,500.00 between 1960 and 1987 and $22,500.00 since 1987. McDonald's has not increased its initial franchise fee to reflect increased sales. For instance, while the franchise fee remained $12,500.00 between 1960 and 1987, the average gross sales of McDonald's restaurants in those years rose from $249,099 to $1,350,000."[7] Not many franchisors, if any, can duplicate these facts.

The court also noted McDonald's refusal to require franchisees to buy equipment and products from the franchisor and McDonald's rules, since 1969, of franchising only one restaurant at a time and refusing territorial agreements.

The court went on to discuss the "system" provided by McDonald's, which included (1) site selection and construction of the physical plant; (2) designs and color schemes for the restaurant and signs; (3) owner/operator, manager, and crew training; (4) equipment layouts; (5) food formulas and specifications; (6) operations specifications, assistance, and monitoring; (7) inventory, accounting and bookkeeping methods; (8) product research and development; and (9) advertising and promotional materials.

This is a reasonably common list of the elements of a franchise system. However, the court's findings of fact go through the specifics of McDonald's behavior with respect to each area. The findings are an incredible tribute to McDonald's attention to detail and to what McDonald's calls QSC, or "quality, service and cleanliness."

[5] *Canterbury, supra* note 1, at 5104.
[6] Id. at 5091.
[7] Id.

The court in *Canterbury* specifically details McDonald's precision standards with respect to the purchase of meats for its hamburgers and emphasizes the expenses incurred in formulating precise computerized procedures for the cooking of french fries.

The court also details the application process and McDonald's "highly regarded training program," goes on to address the franchisor's frequent monitoring of each and every franchise site and the fact that the franchisor has "the largest television advertising budget in the United States to promote a single brand," and then focuses on the operating results of both franchisee-owned and company-owned McDonald's restaurants. It is an awesome story of growth, hard work, and success.

The findings of fact also discuss how difficult it is to obtain a McDonald's franchise. A prospective franchisee can acquire either a new restaurant or an existing restaurant, but there is probably no other franchise as difficult to acquire.

In 1985, when there were some 6,620 operating McDonald's restaurants, 48 new franchisees were granted rights. The court noted that "typically, a new store will meet its projected annualized volume level within the first week of operation."[8] That is remarkable. How many other franchisors can assert and prove such statistics?

The findings of fact also noted that almost always McDonald's controls the real estate, either through direct ownership or subleasing. It is sometimes said that McDonald's is as much in the real estate business as it is in the hamburger business.

Then, in a final showing of the franchisor's power, the court noted two specific instances in which the franchise was withdrawn. Robert Ahern operated a McDonald's restaurant in La Grange, Illinois. McDonald's was dissatisfied with Mr. Ahern's operation and his franchise was terminated. The Golden Arches and all signage or other indicia of McDonald's was removed and Mr. Ahern reopened his restaurant as a hamburger restaurant called Berney's. McDonald's subsequently opened a new restaurant within two blocks of Berney's. Berney's went out of business in less than one year.

Then the court noted:

> Another example involved Eli Schupack. Mr. Schupack operated a McDonald's restaurant in Omaha, Nebraska, from 1965 to 1981. Mr. Schupack was also in the unique position of owning the restaurant premises. McDonald's refused to grant a rewrite to Mr. Schupack and after the franchise expired, the Golden Arches and all signage, trademarks, and trade names identifying the restaurant as a McDonald's were removed. Mr. Schupack reopened the restaurant as "Dodge City Hamburgers" and offered the same type of food products as the former McDonald's restaurant. Mr. Schupack retained his crew, employees and managers. Despite their efforts, sales immediately fell substantially, and the Dodge City Hamburgers restaurant ultimately failed. Subsequent to the closing of Dodge City Hamburgers, McDonald's opened a new restaurant in November 1982 within a few blocks of the former Dodge City Hamburgers restaurant location. Sales at that new McDonald's restaurant during its first full 12 months of operation (December 1982 to November 1983) were $1,212,556,

[8] Id. at 5098.

as compared with sales at Mr. Schupack's McDonald's restaurant during the last 12 full months of its operation (August 1980 to July 1981) of $1,304,541.[9]

§309.3 *The IRS Arguments in* Canterbury

The IRS put forth many theories in *Canterbury* as to why the amount paid was not a "franchise fee" under Code §1253 and therefore not deductible. The arguments were many and weak.

§309.3.1 Franchisor's "Franchisee Fee" for New Franchises Establishes Amount That Can Be Amortized as "Franchise Fee"

The IRS position was that the price McDonald's charged for new franchises ($12,500 during the years at issue) was a "perfect" market which established the value of all McDonald's franchises. The court disagreed, finding that "McDonald's had legitimate and long-standing reasons for charging less than market value for new McDonald's franchises."[10] The court traced this philosophy to Ray Kroc, McDonald's founder, citing his belief that McDonald's should emphasize the long-term relationship with franchisees rather than try to maximize upfront profits—they wanted owner/operators, not investors.

§309.3.2 Purchaser of Operating Franchise May Not Amortize Amount as a Franchise Fee Greater Than Amount Original Franchisee Paid

The IRS argued that, as a matter of law, subsequent franchisees could not amortize an amount greater than the franchise fee paid by the original franchisee. The court found no authority for the IRS position either in the statute or in case law and noted that the IRS failed to cite any. Then the court specifically noted that the IRS's position was directly contrary to a previously published revenue ruling: "Respondent [IRS] has issued a Revenue Ruling that specifically permits a subsequent franchisee to amortize the full price paid for the franchise. Rev. Rul. 88-24, 1988-1 C.B.306."[11]

The court went on to say:

> The fact that the ruling specifically contemplates, and indeed limits, the amount which a subsequent franchisee can amortize, and yet says nothing about limiting that amount to the amount paid by the initial franchisee, gives rise to the inference

[9]Id. at 5099-5100.
[10]Id. at 5100.
[11]Id.

that the subsequent franchisee may amortize the full purchase price of a franchise, even if it exceeds the amount paid by the original franchisee."[12]

The court cited *Jefferson-Pilot Corp. v. Commissioner*[13] and *Tele-Communications, Inc. v. Commissioner*[14] which both allowed subsequent franchisees to amortize franchise costs in excess of the amount paid by the original franchisee.

§309.3.3 Purchaser of Operating Franchise Acquires Other Nonamortizable Assets Such as Goodwill and Large Portion of Purchase Price Should Be Allocated to Those Intangibles

The IRS argued that a large portion of the purchase (to the extent that it exceeds the "franchise fee" originally paid to the franchisor) should be allocated to intangibles such as goodwill.

The court dismissed this argument, effectively saying that the seller of an operating franchise had no goodwill to sell because all these assets belong to the franchisor.

The court phrased the issue as follows:

> A McDonald's franchise encompasses attributes that have traditionally been viewed as non-amortizable goodwill. However, to the extent that these attributes are embodied in the McDonald's franchise, trademarks and trade name, their cost is amortizable under the explicit provisions of Section 1253(d)(2)(A). On the other hand if petitioners acquired intangible assets, such as goodwill, which were not encompassed by or otherwise attributable to the franchise, then a portion of the purchase price should be allocated to such assets.[15]

It was found that there was a tremendous amount of goodwill associated with McDonald's. However, the court felt that it was attributable to the goodwill inherent in the McDonald's system finding that "because of the structure of McDonald's, that goodwill inheres in the McDonald's trade name and trademarks. . . ."

"The rights and benefits conferred by a McDonald's franchise are not assets that the franchisee may use or sell apart from the franchise."[16]

Therefore, the court specifically found that the purchasers acquired no goodwill that was separate and apart from the goodwill inherent in the McDonald's franchise.

Finally, the Tax Reform Act of 1986[17] created Code §1060, which mandates the use of the "residual method" for determining goodwill (see §310 below for further

[12]Id.
[13]98 T.C. 435 (1992).
[14]95 T.C. 495 (1990).
[15]*Canterbury, supra* note 1, at 5101.
[16]Id. at 5101-5102.
[17]Pub. L. No. 99-514, 99th Cong., 2d Sess. (1986 Act).

explanation). Code §1060 may place some limitations on the amount available for such treatment or, at a minimum, require some additional disclosure.

§310 CODE §1060 REQUIREMENTS REGARDING TRANSFERS AND RETRANSFERS

Code §1060, Special Allocation Rules for Certain Asset Acquisition, was added in 1986. Congress enacted Code §1060 primarily for the protection of the IRS. Although there is nothing in its legislative history to suggest that Code §1060 was intended to change the tax treatment with respect to transfers of franchises, nevertheless, under a literal reading, Code §1060 appears to apply to franchise transfers because it requires fundamental changes in the way franchisors and franchisees account for such transfers for tax and financial purposes.

If Code §1060 applies to franchise transfers, a question arises as to whether or not there is a conflict with Code §§1253 and 197, which specifically *do* apply to franchise transfers.

§310.1 Legislative History of Code §1060

The legislative history of Code §1060 is noteworthy. The Committee Reports account of the enactment of Code §1060 reads as follows:

> *Reasons for Change.*—The committee is aware that the allocation of purchase price among the assets of a going business has been a troublesome area of the tax law. Purchase price allocations have been an endless source of controversy between the Internal Revenue Service and taxpayers, principally because of the difficulty of establishing the value of goodwill and going-concern value. The service lacks the resources to challenge allocations to goodwill or going-concern value in all or even a substantial portion of the cases in which it would otherwise assert that the value of those assets are misstated.
>
> The committee believes that it is appropriate to treat the "premium" involved in second-tier allocations as a payment for assets in the nature of goodwill or going-concern value, rather than a payment in excess of the total value of the purchased assets. The committee therefore is requiring taxpayers to apply the residual method in allocating basis to goodwill and going-concern value in all purchases of a going business. The mandatory application of the residual method is also warranted in view of the difficult and uncertain assumptions that are demanded by the application of the formula method and the excessive amount of conflict generated between taxpayer and the Service concerning its application. . . .
>
> The committee is also concerned about the potential for abuse inherent in the sale of a going business where there is no agreement between the parties as to the value of specific assets. In many instances the parties allocation for tax reporting purposes are inconsistent, resulting in a whipsaw of the government. The committee expects that requiring both parties to use the residual method for allocating amounts to nonamortizable goodwill and going-concern value may diminish some of this "whipsaw" potential. The committee has also authorized the Treasury Department to

> require reporting by parties to the sale of a business, so that information reporting may be required regarding amounts allocated to goodwill and going-concern value and to any other categories of assets or specific assets, and such other information as the Secretary deems necessary or appropriate.[1]

There is nothing in the legislative history to suggest that a possible conflict with Code §1253 was considered, nor is there any suggestion that Code §1060 should prevail where it was in conflict with Code §1253.

§310.2 *Allocation of Consideration Under the Residual Method*

The consideration (in this instance the franchise fee) is first to be allocated to Class I assets. Under Temporary Regulations §1.1060-1T(d), Class I assets are cash and cash equivalents. These assets are rarely involved in a franchise transfer. The next item under consideration is the allocation to Class II assets, consisting of certificates of deposit and other readily tradable securities and foreign currencies. These assets are also rarely involved in a franchise transfer.

Class III assets "are all assets (other than Class I, II, and IV assets), both tangible and intangible (whether or not depreciable, depletable, or amortizable), including furniture and fixtures, land, buildings, equipment, accounts receivable, and covenants not-to-compete."[2] After allocating the Class I and Class II assets, all amounts are allocated to specific assets within the Class III category. Any residue is then allocated to Class IV, which includes "intangible assets in the nature of goodwill and going-concern value."[3]

Accordingly, in the context of a normal franchise transfer for a new location to be opened by an original franchisee, practically all of the "sales Price" or "franchise fee" should be allocated to the Class III category.

Form 8594, Asset Acquisition Statement Under Section 1060, as published in July 1990, has four parts. Part I requires the buyer and the seller to provide their addresses and identification numbers, as well as the date of the sale and the total sales price. Part II of the form requires both buyer and seller to determine the aggregate fair market value and allocate the sales price to each of the Class I-IV categories. Questions as to whether the allocation is provided for in some ancillary document (e.g., the contract of sale) or whether the allocation is in conformity with the allocation found in the sales contract must also be answered in Part II. For instance, Part II specifically asks the following question:

> To be completed by buyer only: In connection with the purchase of the group of assets, did you also purchase a license or a covenant not to compete, or enter into a lease agreement, employment contract, management contract, or similar arrangement with the seller (or manager, directors, owners, or employees of the seller)? Yes_____

§310 [1]See Stand. Fed. Tax Rep. (CCH) ¶31,960.90.
[2]Temp. Reg. §1.1060-1T(d)(2)(ii).
[3]Temp. Reg. §1.1060-1T(d)(2)(iii).

No______. If "Yes", specify (a) the type of agreement, and (b) the maximum amount of consideration (not including interest) paid or to be paid under the agreement. (Attach additional sheets if more space is needed).[4]

In the context of the standard initial purchase of a franchise by a franchisee from the franchisor, *if Code §1060 applies to such transaction at all* (see below), it would seem clear that the franchisee is "purchasing" a license (i.e., to use the franchisor's trademark). But how does a franchisee compute the maximum amount of consideration to be paid under the agreement? Does the franchisee include all potential royalty payments to be made over the anticipated life of the franchise? How does the franchisee guess that? How does that information in any way fit in with the purpose of Code §1060?

There is no possibility of the IRS being "whipsawed" in this context. Code §1253, which represents a well-thought-out congressional decision, mandates the treatment the franchisor and the franchisee must give to the transaction. It must be emphasized that under Code §1253, the treatment accorded the franchisor and that accorded the franchisee *do not comport.* There is nothing nefarious in this; it is the specific language of the Code. The franchisor is required to treat the funds as ordinary income, basically, on receipt (however, note the exception to this general rule under Revenue Procedure 71-21, discussed at §§303.1 and 307 above). The initial franchise fee (within limits) is deductible, but only ratably over a 10-year period (or less if the franchise agreement is for a lesser term). Any ongoing royalties paid by the franchisee are deductible as and when paid in accordance with the franchisee's tax accounting method (cash or accrual).

§310.3 Required Reporting and Compliance

A question arises as to whether there is a requirement to file under Code §1060 with respect to the initial sale of a franchise. In terms of the statutory language, the question whether an initial franchise sale is an "applicable asset acquisition" must be answered. Under Code §1060(c), the term "applicable asset acquisition" means "any transfer (whether directly or indirectly) (1) of assets which constitute a trade or business, and (2) with respect to which the transferee's basis in such assets is determined wholly by reference to the consideration paid for such assets."[5]

Temporary Regulations §1.1060-1T(b) attempts to define applicable asset acquisition and illustrates its principles with three examples. In all the examples the applicable asset acquisition involved a transfer of a trade or business that was in operation. An initial transfer of a franchise is not the transfer of an active trade or business; it has no goodwill and no going-concern value at the time of the initial transfer. The store has not yet been opened. Under Temporary Regulations §1.1060-1T(b)(1), a transfer is an applicable asset acquisition if the assets transferred "constitute a trade or business in the hands of either the seller or the purchaser."[6]

[4]See IRS Form 8594, Part II.
[5]Code §1060(c).
[6]Temp. Reg. §1.1060-1T(b)(1).

At the point in time at which there is an initial franchise transfer, it is arguable as to whether there is a trade or business in the hands of either the seller or the purchaser because the franchise transferred is in the "preopening" phase, which has not yet developed into the status of "trade or business." The IRS has frequently used this argument to deny deductions for ordinary and necessary expenses with respect to a trade or business under Code §162. However, practitioners should note that in the situations in which a franchisor is selling an operating company-owned store or an operation that has been acquired from an operating franchisee, this argument would not be available.

Assuming Code §1060 does apply and the parties are required to file Form 8594, it should be acceptable simply to reply on the form that the buyer bought a franchise for a franchise fee plus a royalty.

4

Multiple-Unit Transactions

§401 Multiple-Unit Transactions, Generally
§402 Subfranchising Arrangements
§402.1 Legal and Regulatory Aspects
§402.2 Tax Accounting
§402.3 Financial Accounting
§403 Area Development Agreements
§403.1 Legal and Regulatory Aspects
§403.2 Tax Accounting
§403.3 Financial Accounting
§404 Area Representative Agreements
§404.1 Legal and Regulatory Aspects
§404.2 Tax Accounting
§404.3 Financial Accounting
§405 Brokers
§405.1 Legal and Regulatory Aspects
§405.2 Tax Accounting
§405.3 Financial Accounting

§401 MULTIPLE-UNIT TRANSACTIONS, GENERALLY

Franchisees are not always mom-and-pop operators; often they own many outlets. It is not unheard of for the franchisee to have greater economic power than the franchisor, even though this is not a commonplace occurrence.

Franchisees make more public stock offerings than do franchisors. These large operations, whether or not public companies, enter into several kinds of multiple-unit franchise relationships. Such relationships benefit the franchisee by providing many advantages, such as economies of scale and, possibly, a better deal than a single-unit franchisee could obtain. And, the franchisor obtains a franchisee who will be able to help with the rapid development and expansion of the franchise system.

Generally, these multiple-unit transactions are of four varieties: subfranchising arrangements, area development agreements, area representative agreements, and transactions involving franchise brokers.[1]

§401 [1]Much of this chapter owes its origin to an excellent series of four articles by H. Bret Lowell, which appeared in *Franchise Legal Digest*.

§402 SUBFRANCHISING ARRANGEMENTS

Basically, subfranchising arrangements create two tiers of franchising. On one level the franchisor enters into a relationship with the subfranchisor, which is a franchise relationship for franchise law purposes. This leads to the second level, where the subfranchisor enters into arrangements with subfranchisees who generally operate the sites.

§402.1 *Legal and Regulatory Aspects*

Each relationship, whether franchisor-subfranchisor or subfranchisor-subfranchisee, is a franchise relationship for legal and regulatory purposes. Generally, there is a prospectus requirement at both levels. Each prospectus must comply with the relevant Federal Trade Commission (FTC) and state regulatory requirements.

In these arrangements the actual site operator (the subfranchisee) will generally have a direct contractual relationship only with the subfranchisor. This agreement will normally be the same as any other franchise agreement and will deal with the operation of a single site for the term of the franchise (and possible renewals).

The contract between the franchisor and the subfranchisor normally contains a schedule that requires that a certain number of subfranchises be open within a specified period. Failure to live up to these timetables may cause damages or may even be a default under the agreement. The subfranchisor is generally allowed to find other operators to run the sites or form their own entities to operate as subfranchisees. These agreements address the issues of allocation of royalties and franchise fees and the performance of relevant obligations as a franchisor and subfranchisor.

§402.2 *Tax Accounting*

Each transaction, whether franchisor-subfranchisor or subfranchisor-subfranchisee, is the transfer of a "franchise" for tax purposes and, therefore, is governed by Code §§1253 and 197.

§402.3 *Financial Accounting*

The financial accounting for multiple-unit transactions is generally governed by Statement of Financial Accounting Standards No. 45, *Accounting for Franchise Fee Revenue*, issued in March 1981.

The relevant portion reads as follows:

> 8. Initial franchise fees relating to area franchise sales shall be accounted for following the same principles described in paragraphs 5-7 for individual franchise sales, that is, revenue ordinarily shall be recognized when all material services or conditions relating to the sale(s) have been substantially performed or satisfied by

the franchisor. [The last sentence of paragraph 6 states, "The commencement of operations by the franchisee shall be presumed to be the earliest point at which substantial performance has occurred, unless it can be demonstrated that substantial performance has occurred, (or) unless it can be demonstrated that substantial performance of all obligations, including services rendered voluntarily, has occurred before that time."] If the franchisor's substantial obligations under the franchise agreement relate to the area franchise and do not depend significantly on the number of individual franchises to be established, substantial performance shall be determined using the same criteria applicable to individual franchisees (paragraph 5). However, if the franchisor's substantial obligations depend on the number of individual franchises established within the area, area franchise fees shall be recognized in proportion to the initial mandatory services provided. Revenue that may have to be refunded because future services are not performed shall not be recognized by the franchisor until the franchisee has no right to receive a refund.

9. The substance of an area franchise agreement shall determine when material services or conditions relating to a sale have been substantially performed or satisfied. Sometimes, the efforts and total cost relating to initial services are not affected significantly by the number of outlets opened in an area and, therefore, the area franchise sale is similar to an individual franchise sale. Conversely, when the efforts and total cost relating to initial services are affected significantly by the number of outlets opened in an area, it may be necessary to regard the franchise agreement as a divisible contract and estimate the number of outlets involved so that revenue may be recognized in proportion to the outlets for which the required services have been substantially performed. Estimates shall consider the anticipated number of outlets based on the terms of the franchise agreement (for example, time limitations and any specified minimum or maximum number of outlets). Any change in estimate resulting from a change in circumstances shall result in recognizing remaining fees as revenue in proportion to remaining services to be performed.[1]

§403 AREA DEVELOPMENT AGREEMENTS

An area development agreement is basically an agreement between a franchisor and a franchisee who is buying a large territory that will support a number of outlets. Generally, each site opened by an area developer will be owned by the area developer (though possibly through several entities, usually a separate entity is used for each site to obtain limited liability). Often an area development agreement includes a performance schedule that obligates the area developer to open a certain number of sites within a specific amount of time.

§403.1 *Legal and Regulatory Aspects*

In an area development arrangement, there is only one level of franchise relationship: that between the franchisor and the area developer. The prospectus (which will be required to include both the franchise agreement and the area

§402 [1]Statement of Financial Accounting Standards No. 45, Accounting for Franchise Fee Revenues (March 1981).

development agreement) will generally subject only the franchisor to FTC and state filing requirements. The franchisor usually requires that each of the area developer's sites be subject to a separate franchise agreement.

§403.2 *Tax Accounting*

From the franchisor's point of view, the franchise fee, an upfront portion of the payment from the area developer, is ordinary income when received (i.e., it does not include the income received from the sale of capital assets) (see Chapter 3). Likewise, for tax purposes, the receipt by the franchisor of contingent payments or royalties is income when received or accrued.

From the area developer's point of view, its payments are governed by Code §§1253(d) and 197. As discussed in Chapter 3, the upfront payments are generally deductible over a 10-, 15-, or 25-year period, depending on the law in effect at the time of the transaction, whereas the contingent payments are currently deductible in accordance with the taxpayer's method of accounting.

In the area development context, particular attention must be given to the $100,000 limitation on amortization of the upfront payment found in the former Code §1253(d)(2)(B). That limitation applies to "all payments which are part of the same transaction (or a series of related transactions)." For a detailed discussion of this limitation see §304.2 above. The language would seem to impose the $100,000 amortization limitation on area development agreements with upfront payments in excess of $100,000. However, a strong argument can be made that the limit was meant to apply to a single-site payment of more than $100,000 and that the "same transaction" language, as quoted above, is merely the normal congressional attempt to telescope sham transactions. This issue has not yet been the subject of any reported court decisions.

§403.3 *Financial Accounting*

In general, it would appear that the treatment of an area development agreement should be governed by Statement of Financial Accounting Standards No. 45, particularly paragraphs 8 and 9, quoted at §402.3 above. However, in an attempt to record such income as quickly as possible (to help with current earnings), some franchisors have taken the position that certain payments on area development agreements are not subject to the general rule that "[t]he commencement of operations by the franchisee shall be presumed to be the earliest point at which substantial performance has occurred"[1] and the upfront payments shall be treated as income upon receipt. This is discussed in greater detail in the Appendix.

§403 [1]Statement of Financial Accounting Standards No. 45, Accounting for Franchise Fee Revenues (March 1981), ¶6.

§404 AREA REPRESENTATIVE AGREEMENTS

In the area representative's situation, a franchisor enters into an agreement with an area representative in which the area representative helps market the franchises within the area, and generally performs some of the assistance and supervisory functions of the franchisor.

The area representative agreement usually includes a performance timetable, which requires the area representative to provide a certain number of "qualified prospects" to become franchisees within a specified period. The agreement will further provide that the area representative will be entitled to certain percentages of the franchise fee and the continuing royalty.

§404.1 *Legal and Regulatory Aspects*

For franchise purposes, whether or not the agreement between the franchisor and the area representative is a franchise agreement is an unanswered question. The answer depends on the specific terms of the agreement. Generally, prudent counsel will not rely on possible technical distinctions and will advise the franchisor to file the area representative agreement as well.

When the franchisor's obligations under the franchise agreement are performed by the area representative, that fact must be disclosed to the franchisee in the franchise prospectus. For franchise law purposes, although the agreement between the franchisor and the franchisee is a "franchise" subject to FTC rules as well as the various state regulatory requirements, the area representative is not generally a party to the franchise arrangement.

§404.2 *Tax Accounting*

The tax treatment or revenues in the area representative context, though not yet the subject of any case or regulation, should be no different from the economics of the situation. The franchisor receives ordinary income to the extent of its share of the franchise fee and royalty income. The area representative is similarly treated with respect to its portion of the receipts.

From the franchisee's point of view, the payments are made in accordance with the franchise agreement and are therefore subject to the Code §§1253 and 197 rules as if there were no interjection of an area representative.

§404.3 *Financial Accounting*

Area representatives are sometimes required to pay an upfront fee in order to become the area representative. Sometimes the agreement will only provide for payments to the area representative upon the signing of franchisees. If the upfront payment is not required, it will not be an issue with respect to financial accounting. However, if an upfront fee from the area representative is required, the same financial accounting issues may arise as in the area development context (see §403.3 above and the Appendix).

§405 BROKERS

Franchise brokers are not substantially different from stockbrokers. They are commission salesmen.

§405.1 Legal and Regulatory Aspects

For franchise law purposes, there is no requirement that the relationship between the franchisor and the broker be described in the prospectus. However, in most situations there are disclosure and registration requirements imposed upon the franchisor that uses a franchise broker.

§405.2 Tax Accounting

From a tax accounting point of view, a franchise broker is treated in a similar manner as a "broker" in any other context (such as a broker selling real estate or stock and bonds). Brokers are paid on the basis of the cost of the sale which comes from the total selling price. From the franchisee's point of view it makes no difference whether the franchisor pays or uses a broker. The franchisee's cost basis is the total amount paid which is subject to Code §1253(d) rules.

§405.3 Financial Accounting

For financial accounting purposes, payments to a franchise broker raise no special issues and are treated in the same manner as other payments to other brokers.

5

Pooled Advertising Funds

§501 Purpose of the Funds
§502 IRS Position
§502.1 The Seven-Up Company
§502.2 *Ford Dealers Advertising Fund Co.*—The Issue Resurrected
§502.3 Nonacquiescence: Revenue Rulings 74-318, 74-319
§502.4 Continued Litigation—*Insty-Prints,* etc.
§503 Tax Status of the Fund
§503.1 Form of the Fund Entity
§503.2 Is the Fund a Separate Taxpayer?
§504 Payments to the Fund
§504.1 Are Payments to the Fund Income for Tax Purposes?
§504.2 Are Payments Deductible for Tax Purposes?
§505 Planning Considerations
§506 Alternative Defense
§507 Conclusion

§501 PURPOSE OF THE FUNDS

Advertising, primarily systemwide and uniform, often lies at the heart of a successful franchise operation. It is one of the synergies of the franchisor-franchisee relationship. Systemwide advertising is far more productive and valuable than the aggregation of individual franchisee programs.

Frequently, franchisors require that franchisees pay a certain percentage of gross proceeds toward a common (i.e., systemwide) advertising program. In this manner, the small entrepreneur (the franchisee) gains access to the mass media with its powerful ability to utilize the franchise's image to its advantage.

The operation of pooled advertising programs involves collecting, holding, and disbursing the advertising monies. The participants may include the franchisee, the franchisor, systemwide suppliers, or advertising campaign joint ventures. The advertising fund's basic purpose is to administer the advertising fee collections that create advertising programs. These programs are designed to build sales and enhance the chain's identity. Moreover, resources are pooled to obtain critical mass media buys and to create marketing and advertising materials for franchisees.

The tax aspects of pooled advertising funds raise four basic questions:

(1) Do payments to the fund constitute income for tax purposes? And, if so, to whom?
(2) What is the tax status of the fund? Is it a separate taxpayer? If so, is it classified as a trust, an association taxable as corporation, or a ledger account on the franchisor's books?
(3) Are payments into the fund deductible, and, if so, when?
(4) If the fund earns money before it is disbursed for advertising, what is the status of such earnings?

§502 IRS POSITION

The taxability of pooled advertising program receipts has been an issue for a long time. Following is a history of the IRS position on the issue.

§502.1 *The Seven-Up Company*

The landmark case testing the taxability of pooled advertising is *Seven-Up Company v. Commissioner.*[1] The events at issue in *Seven-Up* centered around a national advertising program begun in 1943. The case was decided correctly in 1950.

The scenario of *Seven-Up* is as follows. The taxpayer was the Seven-Up Company, which franchised bottling distributorships with each bottler having an exclusive territory. Before the adoption of the national campaign, each franchisee was responsible for the advertising within its own territory subject to the advice and input from the franchisor. A national campaign was begun with participating bottlers contributing a fee based on the number of gallons of extract purchased from the franchisor. The payments were made directly to the franchisor. It is not clear from the record just who had actual control over the fund—the franchisee, the franchisor, or both—but all monies were paid to and disbursed by the franchisor. In addition, all the advertising was placed through a single agency.

In its opinion, the Tax Court emphasized the role and input of the franchisees and, more specifically, noted that the advertising agency reported annually to the franchisees.[2] The Tax Court held that the franchisor was not taxable on receipt of the contributions to the pooled advertising fund from the franchisees; the IRS acquiesced.[3]

In 1951, the IRS litigated an analogous issue in *Broadcast Measurement Bureau, Inc. v. Commissioner.*[4] The Tax Court ruled against the IRS position, and once again the IRS acquiesced.[5] The issue was not challenged for 16 years.

§502 [1]14 T.C. 965 (1950).
[2]Id. at 973.
[3]1950-2 C.B. 4.
[4]16 T.C. 988 (1951).
[5]1951-2 C.B. 2.

§502.2 Ford Dealers Advertising Fund Co.—*The Issue Resurrected*

In 1967, the IRS chose to litigate once again. In *Angelus Funeral Home v. Commissioner,*[6] it disputed a similar issue and, once again, the taxpayer prevailed. In 1970, the IRS tried the same issue two more times.[7] The taxpayers prevailed twice more.

In 1971, the IRS bought its position before the Tax Court and the court held that though the form at issue was somewhat different from that in *Seven-Up,* the substance was the same. In *Ford Dealers Advertising Fund Co., Inc. v. Commissioner,*[8] the Tax Court rejected the IRS position; that decision was affirmed on appeal.[9]

It should be noted that in *Ford,* the program was administered by a separate corporation which had its membership restricted to Ford dealers in the Jacksonville, Florida, area. Once the dealers became members, they authorized Ford to add amounts to the advertising fund. These amounts were labeled as contributions on the invoices sent for cars and trucks purchased. The payments were made directly to Ford but were paid over to the program administrator.

It has been argued that the IRS decided to appeal *Ford* after 21 years of court defeats because of the explosive growth that franchising had experienced since the *Seven-Up* decision.[10] Whatever spurred the IRS zeal, it is clear that defeat only served to stimulate its ardor.

§502.3 *Nonacquiescence: Revenue Rulings 74-318, 74-319*

In 1974, the IRS refocused the essence of its contentions and once again went on the attack. The IRS issued a nonacquiescence (i.e., it refused to follow a specific court decision[11]) in *Ford.*[12] Then the IRS formulated Revenue Ruling 74-318, with facts clearly taken from *Ford* but reaching the opposite result.[13] In addition, the IRS withdrew its acquiescence in *Seven-Up* and substituted an acquiescence in result only.[14] With respect to *Broadcast Measurement Bureau,* it withdrew its acquiescence and substituted a nonacquiescence.[15]

The IRS's new position was that payments for advertising to a separate entity organized for that purpose are gross income to such entity. To carry this position to what it deemed its logical conclusion, the IRS issued Revenue Ruling 74-319,[16]

[6]47 T.C. 391 (1967), *aff'd,* 407 F.2d 210 (9th Cir. 1969), 69-1 U.S.T.C. ¶9216, *cert. denied,* 396 U.S. 824.

[7]Dri-Power Distribs. Assn. Trust v. Commissioner, 54 T.C. 460 (1970); New York State Assn. of Real Estate Bds. Group Ins. Fund v. Commissioner, 54 T.C. 1325 (1970).

[8]456 F.2d 255 (5th Cir. 1972), 55 T.C. 761 (1971).

[9]456 F.2d 255 (5th Cir. 1972), 72-1 U.S.T.C. ¶9228, *aff'g per curiam* 55 T.C. 761.

[10]James, Federal Income Tax Issues in Franchise Advertising Programs, 2 Franchising (ABA) 7 (Spring 1982).

[11]The IRS is bound to follow only decisions of the U.S. Supreme Court.

[12]1974-2 C.B. 5.

[13]1974-2 C.B. 14.

[14]1974-2 C.B. 4.

[15]Id.

[16]1974-2 C.B. 15.

holding that the existence of a separate entity may be inferred if a franchisor receives contributions for a pooled advertising fund from franchisees (such entity, of course, being taxable upon receipt of payments for advertising).

§502.4 *Continued Litigation*—Insty-Prints, *etc.*

The IRS has not persuaded any court with respect to its position, yet the continuous defeats do not seem to have dissuaded it. The IRS has continued to press its contentions in *Florist's Transworld Delivery Association,*[17] *Greater Pittsburgh Chrysler Dealers Association,*[18] *North Carolina Oil Jobbers Association, Inc.,*[19] and most recently in the case of *Frank and Freida Schochet, Trustees of Insty-Prints, Inc., National Advertising Fund Trust,*[20] and it has lost every time. Nonetheless, no acquiescences have been issued.

A review of *Insty-Prints* is informative and in order. A headnote synopsis of the case reads:

> Petitioner is organized to collect monthly payments from franchisees of Insty-Prints, Inc., which payments are to be used solely for the advertising and promotion of the Insty-Prints business. Petitioner also earned interest on payments which were not currently expended by it. *Held:* payments received by petitioner for advertising and promotion are not income to petitioner. *Ford Dealers Advertising Fund, Inc., v. Commissioner* [Dec. 30,654], 55 T.C. 761 (1971), affd. per curiam [72-1 U.S.T.C. ¶9228] 456 F.2d 255 (5th Cir. 1972) and *Seven-Up v. Commissioner,* 14 T.C. 965 (1950) followed. *Held further*: Interest earned by petitioner is income. *Held further*: Petitioner is not entitled to deductions for advertising disbursements.[21]

The Tax Court upheld the precedent with respect to the issue whether or not income is received. However, two other issues were left unresolved. The last footnote of the case reads: "We express no opinion as to whether petitioner would be entitled to a deduction for advertising payments made from interest income."[22]

§503 TAX STATUS OF THE FUND

The tax status of the fund is determined by the form of the fund entity. The discussion that follows addresses that issue.

[17]67 T.C. 333 (1976).
[18]77-1 U.S.T.C. ¶9293 (D. Pa. 1977).
[19]78-2 U.S.T.C. ¶9658 (D. N.C. 1978).
[20]44 T.C.M. 556, T.C. Memo. 1982-416.
[21]Id.
[22]Id. at 568 n.28.

§503.1 *Form of the Fund Entity*

The type of entity used to administer the pooled advertising fund also becomes a determinative factor. In *Insty-Prints,* the taxpayer was a trust formed under Minnesota law, and the husband and wife, acting as trustees of the fund, were also principals of the franchisor.

The court's opinion revealed the following facts:

> Insty-Prints sold its first franchise sometime around October 1966. Under the typical Insty-Prints franchise agreement, a franchise is granted covering [a] limited geographic area for 10 years (with an automatic 10-year renewal period unless notification of nonrenewal is made by either party) which allows the franchisee the right to use the trade name "Insty-Prints" and conduct an Insty-Prints business at a single location within the franchise area. The franchisor, Insty-Prints, is obligated to provide specified initial advice and training in the conduct of an Insty-Prints shop and specific continuing services to each franchisee. The franchisee is required to adopt and maintain certain business procedures and conduct a high-quality shop in accordance with Insty-Prints' standards. Insty-Prints receives three cents for each dollar of gross sales of the franchisee as a royalty.[1]

This is a standard set of facts with respect to business format franchisors. The court further stated:

> The required payments to the Insty-Prints national advertising fund began in 1969 and were received by Insty-Prints, which created a separate ledger account for such payments on its corporate books. Insty-Prints segregated the advertising funds in a separate bank account. The advertising funds continued to be paid to Insty-Prints until 1973.
>
> On November 23, 1973, a trust agreement establishing the Insty-Prints National Advertising Fund (petitioner) was entered into by Insty-Prints, as grantor, and Frank and Freida Schochet, as trustees.[2]

The court noted that the trustee had no duty to inquire as to the purposes of any disbursements or any responsibility for disbursements made in accordance with instructions from the Insty-Prints advertising committee. Moreover, the beneficiaries of the trust were all the Insty-Prints franchisees and the company-owned stores. The trust itself had no employees. The franchisor provided all the necessary services to the trust, which included paying all its administrative expenses. The trust did not own or lease any real or personal property. The court's recitation of the facts continued as follows:

> Insty-Prints included receipts from franchisees for advertising as income in 1969 and 1970, pursuant to the advice of its accountants. Insty-Prints retained a different accounting firm sometime in 1970 and was advised by that firm that its prior accounting for advertising fund receipts was incorrect. Insty-Prints accordingly filed a refund

§503 [1]Frank and Freida Schochet, Trustees of Insty-Prints, Inc. National Advertising Fund Trust, 44 T.C.M. 556, 557, T.C. Memo. 1982-416.

[2]Id. at 558.

claim which the Internal Revenue Service allowed. Petitioner filed no tax return, nor did Insty-Prints file a corporate tax return, which included in income the $847.47 of franchisee payments made after September 30, 1979, and the $420.35 of interest earned on the advertising fund in 1970. Petitioner did not file any returns for 1971 nor 1972, nor did Insty-Prints file corporate income tax returns for the years ended September 30, 1971, and September 30, 1972, which included in income any contributions made to the advertising fund. Petitioner has filed no returns for the years 1973, 1974 and 1975.

In the statutory notice of deficiency dated March 20, 1979, respondent determined that the monies received from Insty-Prints franchisees for the advertising fund and interest were gross income. Respondent further determined that petitioner's advertising expenses are deductible as provided by section 277 [footnotes omitted].[3]

The petitioner (in this case, the trust which the IRS refused to stipulate was a trust for federal income tax purposes) asserted that the payments by the franchisees to the fund were held in trust for a specific purpose and, therefore, were not gross income. It maintained a similar position with respect to the interest received by the fund.

The IRS argued that the fund was taxable as an association (i.e., a corporation for tax purposes) and, therefore, had to include in income the payments it received from its franchisee-members. It argued further that the *Seven-Up* case and its progeny, on which the taxpayer relied in its argument, were incorrectly decided.

In the *Insty-Prints* case the Tax Court reviewed *Seven-Up*, explaining its reasoning as follows:

The payments made by the participating bottlers [in *Seven-Up*] were not for services rendered or to be rendered by petitioner. Neither were they part of the purchase price of the extract. They did not, therefore, constitute *earnings* received by petitioner under a claim received by petitioner under a claim of right and without restriction as to disposition, which petitioner would have had to include in its gross income under the rule laid down in *North American Oil Consolidated v. Burnet*, 286 U.S. 417. While petitioner had the right to receive the bottlers' contributions under its agreements with them, all the facts and circumstances surrounding the transaction clearly indicate that it was the intention of all parties concerned that these contributions were to be used to acquire national advertising for the 7-Up bottled beverage and for that purpose only, and that petitioner was to be a conduit for passing on the funds contributed to the advertising agency which was to arrange for and supply the national advertising. *Cf. Central Life Assurance Society, Mutual v. Commissioner*, 51 Fed. (2d) 939. Although the funds were not all expended in the year received, for reasons set forth in our findings, petitioner did expend them for national advertising, did not use them for general corporate purposes, treated the amounts on hand in the fund on its books as a liability to the bottlers, and considered itself, as evidenced by its letter of May 2, 1944, to one of the participating bottlers merely as a trustee, handling the bottlers' money. [14 T.C. at 977-978.][4]

[3]Id. at 562.

[4]Id. at 562-563.

§503.2 *Is the Fund a Separate Taxpayer?*

The court's decision was broad. It held that the legal classification of the pooled advertising fund (i.e., whether the fund is organized as a bookkeeping account, a trust, or an association) was immaterial and if the franchisee payments are sufficiently restricted as to use, they are not gross income. The court chastised the IRS for placing undue emphasis on the words "trustee" and "agent" in prior decisions, making clear that their use of terms such as "trustee," "agent," and "conduit" served for purposes of analogy only and did not speak to the requirements of any specific legal relationship.

§504 PAYMENTS TO THE FUND

There are several planning considerations taxpayers must take into account when making payments to the fund. In the discussion that follows, the determination of whether these payments are income or deductible for tax purposes is addressed.

§504.1 *Are Payments to the Fund Income for Tax Purposes?*

After finally settling the issues,[1] the Tax Court in *Insty-Prints* went on to muddy the waters by saying: "Nothing before us indicates the manner in which the Insty-Prints franchisees treated their payments to Insty-Prints, and, later, to petitioner. The case of the deductibility of such payments is not before us and we express no opinion thereupon."[2]

Further, the court discovered that in each year the taxpayer made advertising disbursements, the sum of accumulated and current franchisee payments exceeded the advertising disbursements from the fund. Therefore, the court held that because the trustees were allowed to use the interest earned on the fund to employ agents, pay expenses, or resolve claims, the interest earned was income.

The court noted that in several previous cases the fund, although not treating contributions as income, had nonetheless earned interest on the advances which were reported as income. In *Florists' Transworld Delivery Association,*[3] *Ford Dealers Advertising Fund, Inc.,*[4] *New York State Association of Real Estate Boards Group Insur-*

§504 [1]"Accordingly, we find that the classification of petitioner as an association is irrelevant to our present purpose and we adhere to and reaffirm our holding in *Seven-Up Co.*" Frank and Freida Schochet, Trustees of Insty Prints, Inc. National Advertising Fund Trust, 44 T.C.M. 556, 565, T.C. Memo. 1982-416.

[2]Id. at 566.

[3]Florist's Transworld Delivery Assn. v. Commissioner, 67 T.C. 333 (1976), *acq.* 1978-2 C.B. 2, *nonacq.* 1978-2 C.B. 3.

[4]456 F.2d 255 (5th Cir. 1972), 72-1 U.S.T.C. ¶9228.

ance Fund,[5] and *Angelus Funeral Home,*[6] each taxpayer earned interest on the advances and the interest was reported as income.

§504.2 *Are Payments Deductible for Tax Purposes?*

It seems clear that if payments to the fund are not income for tax purposes, the subsequent expenditures made for advertising are not deductible to the fund.

The payments by the franchisees, and possibly the franchisor for company-owned stores, at first blush would appear to qualify as ordinary and necessary business expenses deductible under Code §162. However, it is now fairly clear under the proposed regulations[7] recently released by the IRS that payments to such an advertising fund are not deductible until expended by the fund. Therefore, it may be prudent for a franchisor to issue correspondence at least annually to franchisees informing them that only a specified percentage of contributions to the fund appears to be deductible in the current year.

§505 PLANNING CONSIDERATIONS

In spite of its consistent failure, the IRS has yet to acquiesce in decisions concluding that franchisee payments to a pooled advertising fund are not income to the fund. Therefore, the prudent taxpayer must assume an attack by the IRS to be a potential risk. In light of the costs attendant upon any contest with the IRS, good planning requires staying as close to favorable precedent as possible.

The first issue to be considered in designing a pooled advertising campaign for a franchisor is the structure to be adopted. The franchisor itself can collect, administer, and disburse the funds. In addition, a trust, corporation, or some other entity owned or controlled, in whole or in part, by the franchisees can be used.

This decision should be made primarily on the basis of business considerations. In *Insty-Prints,* the format was changed during the course of operations from a book entry on the franchisor's books to a trust entity. This was done without changing the basic franchise agreement or prospectus. Therefore, it is clear that a franchisor should adopt a different procedure.

The Tax Court said, "We agree with petitioner that whether the fund is organized as a bookkeeping account, a trust, or an association, if the franchisee payments are sufficiently restricted as to use, they are not gross income."[1] However, using a separate entity appears more prudent because:

[5] 54 T.C. 1325 (*nonacq.*) (1974).

[6] Angelus Funeral Home v. Commissioner, 47 T.C. 391 (1967), *aff'd,* 407 F.2d 210 (9th Cir. 1969), 69-1 U.S.T.C. ¶9216, *cert. denied,* 396 U.S. 824.

[7] See Prop. Reg. §1.461-4.

§505 [1] Frank and Freida Schochet, Trustees of Insty-Prints, Inc. National Advertising Fund Trust, 44 T.C.M. 556, T.C. Memo. 1982-416, at 980.

(1) It substantially reduces the likelihood of the sponsor's being deemed taxable;
(2) If interest is earned that is to be taxable, it can be taxable to a separate entity presumably at a lower tax rate; and
(3) The documents executed in forming the separate entity can be used to memorialize the filing position.

On the other hand, using a separate entity carries certain problems because:

(1) It clearly adds to the IRS argument that the recipient of the fund contributions is a separate entity; and
(2) It seems to enhance the IRS argument slightly that such separate entity must be taxable because it does not qualify as an exempt organization under any provision of the Code.

In either case, a review of the many court decisions shows that a large percentage requires three elements to hold that the contributions to the fund are not gross income:

(1) The contributions are not payments for products or services provided by the sponsor or the entity;
(2) The recipient of the contributions is subject to clear restrictions as to what purposes funds can be expended for; and
(3) The recipient is under a clear obligation to spend the funds.

Clearly, sound planning requires a written agreement embodying all the rights and obligations of the parties. Franchise operations that have been successful without implementing such written agreements should not hesitate to reduce recordkeeping and accountability to the franchisees. Additionally, it is probably wise to obligate the fund to expend surplus interest earned as well as to expend its contributions.

Some of the drafting points that should be considered when completing the necessary documents are as follows:

(1) The governing instrument for the advertising fund should *expressly* restrict the use of funds and income thereon solely to advertising purposes;
(2) Documents should clearly state that no profit, gain, or other benefit shall inure to the franchisor;
(3) Contributions to the fund should be segregated from the franchisor's corporate assets and treated separately for accounting purposes;
(4) The governing instruments should require that no contributions to the fund or income thereon can revert back to the franchisees or the franchisor prior to termination of the fund;
(5) The documents should allow occasional contributions by the franchisor as long as they are subject to the same restrictions on use of franchisee contributions; and
(6) Franchisees should be given some role in administration of the fund and

accountability through reporting of fund activity by the franchisor or the fund itself.

Of course, once the proper agreements are executed, the fund must also be administered within the principles of case precedent.

There are also some operational considerations that should be made to minimize tax risks. If the IRS is ever successful in arguing that the fund should be taxed on its income, the IRS will be forced to allow ordinary and necessary business expenses deductible against the alleged taxable income. Therefore, the fund should maximize the extent to which receipts into the fund are expended or specifically committed in the fiscal period in which they are received.

§506 ALTERNATIVE DEFENSE

Revenue Procedure 71-21[1] provides for the deferral of income received "substantially for services" to be performed in the next succeeding tax year. As an alternative defense, if the IRS was successful in substantiating its current position, the franchise advertising fund of the franchisor could determine that the income received by the fund was substantially for services to be performed in the current and succeeding tax year, thus allowing the fund to defer the income received until those advertising services are performed. This would normally occur in the subsequent tax year, thereby eliminating any liability. Clearly, the most difficult point to argue under this theory is that the income was received "substantially for services," because the fund may not be deemed to be providing services within the meaning of the revenue procedure. This position under these circumstances has not been tested in the courts.

§507 CONCLUSION

Because of the enormous growth of franchising and the pooled advertising funds it generates, great care must be given to the selection and the operation of the appropriate vehicle to supervise the fund. For the protection of all, specific restraints and obligations must be memorialized in clear written form to insure that the fund's advertising dollars are not dissipated by mistakenly causing the contributions to become taxable receipts.

§506 [1]1971-2 C.B. 549.

6

Passive "Royalty" Income: Personal Holding Company and S Corporation Considerations

§601 Passive "Royalty" Income, Generally
§602 Personal Holding Companies
§602.1 Statutory Requirements
§602.2 Legislative Purpose and History
§602.3 Case Law—Franchising
§602.4 Case Law—"Compensation for Services" Versus "Royalty Income"
§602.5 Recommendations
§603 S Corporations

§601 PASSIVE "ROYALTY" INCOME, GENERALLY

If a successful corporate franchisor is a closely held regular corporation (under certain attribution tests), certain negative tax aspects can attach to the receipt of payments denominated royalties. Such payments can constitute personal holding company income and thereby subject a regular corporation to a penalty tax on its undistributed earnings—the personal holding company tax.[1] Also, the payments formerly could be characterized as passive investment income, thereby subjecting an S corporation to a penalty tax and/or the termination of its S election.[2] This potential pitfall has, however, been removed by a change in the IRS regulations in 1992.

§602 PERSONAL HOLDING COMPANIES

The example below illustrates the intricacies of the application of the franchise rules to personal holding companies (PHCs).

§601 [1]Code §541; Reg. §1.541-1.
[2]Code §1362(d)(3).

EXAMPLE

Roman Lobe, Inc. is a Texas corporation wholly owned by Ralph and Edna Stuckey. Several years ago, in their hometown of Laredo, the Stuckeys opened and operated their first Roman Lobe ear piercing salon using their new select Staab process for painless piercing. They developed and refined a distinctive business format. When Ralph and Edna's operation had grown to four stores, they decided that the best opportunity for growth would be to franchise their know-how and ideas and trademark their distinct format. By 1990, the Stuckeys had their company-owned-and-operated centers and 46 Roman Lobe franchise outlets.

Under the Roman Lobe franchise agreement, a franchisee is obligated to pay an initial franchise fee of $25,000 plus an ongoing royalty equal to 6 percent of gross revenues from piercing. For its 1990 fiscal year, Roman Lobe filed a federal tax return showing the following:

(1) Income from operations (4 stores @ $250,000 per store)	$1,000,000
(2) Franchise fees (10 stores @ $25,000 each)	$ 250,000
(3) Royalties (46 stores which average $1,667,000 per site @ 6% yield approximately $100,000 per store)	$4,600,000
Total gross income	$5,850,000

Roman Lobe paid the Stuckeys each $250,000 for fiscal year 1990 and spent another $1.35 million on operating overhead. Accordingly, Roman Lobe showed taxable income equal to $4 million ($5.85 million gross income, less $500,000 for Ralph and Edna's salary, less $1.35 million operating overhead expenses). Roman Lobe paid its income taxes in accordance with the then current tax rates. Roman Lobe paid no dividends for fiscal year 1990. To promote its business and national recognition, Roman Lobe invested the entire corporate capital remaining after taxes to build the world's first Piercetorium and Staaborama.

Roman Lobe was selected for audit by the IRS, and, after careful inspection, the revenue agents determined that Roman Lobe was entitled to every deduction it took. However, after reviewing Roman Lobe's operations and revenue sources, the IRS determined that the royalties collected constituted PHC income and that Roman Lobe was a PHC and, therefore, issued a notice of deficiency to Roman Lobe stating that Roman Lobe was liable for the PHC tax for its fiscal year 1990.

§602.1 Statutory Requirements

Code §541, Imposition of Personal Holding Company Tax, for the year at issue reads:

> In addition to other taxes imposed by this chapter, there is hereby imposed for each taxable year on the undistributed personal holding company income (as defined in section 545) of every personal holding company (as defined in section 542) a personal holding company tax equal to 28 percent . . . of the undistributed personal holding company income.

Code §542 defines a PHC as a corporation that meets two tests:

(1) an income test—if at least 60 percent of the corporation's adjusted ordinary gross income in the taxable year is personal holding company income; and
(2) a stock ownership test—if at any time during the last half of the taxable year more than 50 percent of the corporation's stock is owned by five or fewer individuals (with certain attribution rules).

Code §543 defines PHC income as income from any one of eight specific categories. The category relevant for this discussion is in Code §543(a)(1), "Dividends, etc.—Dividends, interest, *royalties* (other than mineral, oil or gas royalties or copyright royalties), and annuities" (emphasis added).

The pertinent part of Reg. §1.543-1(b)(3) reads as follows: "The term 'royalties' (other than mineral, oil, or gas royalties or certain copyright royalties) includes amounts received for the privilege of using patents, copyrights, secret processes and formulas, goodwill, trademarks, trade brands, *franchises,* and other like property" (emphasis added).

In the Roman Lobe example, it would appear that Roman Lobe is liable for the PHC tax. Ralph and Edna own all of Roman Lobe's shares so the stock ownership test is met. The "royalties" of $4.6 million reported on the return constituted 78 percent of the adjusted ordinary gross income of $5.85 million. It would appear that more than 60 percent of adjusted ordinary gross income was PHC income.

To illustrate the potential scope of this problem, let us assume another fact in this example. In 1988, the Stuckeys had an initial public offering and took Roman Lobe public. After the successful offering there were 750 shareholders in the corporation (some of which were brokers holding the stock in street name) but the Stuckeys retained 51 percent of the corporation. Nonetheless, if the income test is met, the stock ownership test would still classify Roman Lobe as a PHC—even though it is publicly held and traded. Thus, closely held in the PHC context does not apply only to family enterprises.

How can a successful franchisor effectively confront such a predicament?

§602.2 *Legislative Purpose and History*

In order to evolve a strategy for dealing with the PHC tax, it is useful to analyze the legislative purpose and history underlying its present provisions.

In terms of understanding the legislative policy aspects, one must be prepared to deal with at least two basic legal issues:

(1) the general tax law issue of characterizing active business income and passive investment income; and
(2) the difficulty which courts have in characterizing the franchisor-franchisee relationship. Although clearly different from the master-servant or employer-employee relationship with which the law is familiar, it is also something other than the standard independent contractor relationship.

The purpose of the PHC tax, originally enacted in 1934, significantly strengthened in 1937 and again in 1964, was quite simple. It was enacted as a drastic penalty tax focused primarily on the perceived evil referred to as the incorporated pocketbook. When the PHC tax was first passed in 1934, the maximum individual tax bracket was 63 percent and the maximum corporate tax rate was 13.75 percent—a difference of 49.25 percent. In 1936 and 1937, the maximum individual rates were 64 percent less. Accordingly, it became clear to many wealthy taxpayers that they should incorporate their investment assets rather than hold them individually because incorporation meant subjecting the income earned to the much lower corporate tax rates and permitting increased accumulation of wealth.

The PHC tax was enacted to impose a stiff penalty tax on such "incorporated pocketbooks" and to combat other certain abuses, including "incorporated yachts" and "incorporated talents." The penalty was imposed mechanically.

It should be noted that in 1990, the year of our example, the top individual tax rate was 28 percent and the maximum corporate rate was 34 percent—a 6 percent differential *in favor of the individual rates.* Now the maximum rates are 35 percent corporate and 39.6 percent individual. Thus, clearly, it no longer pays to incorporate a pocketbook. However, even though the tax abuse the PHC tax was enacted to combat no longer exists, the penalty lingers on as a trap for the unwary.

Congress did not intend to interfere with active income from legitimate operating businesses when it enacted the PHC tax. However, it adopted such mechanical PHC income tests that interference was inevitable—precluded over the years only by congressional response to industry-specific persuasion.

An eminent authority has traced the history of this issue:

> From the inception of the personal holding company tax, banks, life insurance companies and surety companies were . . . recognized as active businesses, and were excluded from the personal holding company provision. Thereafter, a steady procession of supplicants has been granted relief by Congress for comparable reasons: holders of mineral, oil or gas royalties (in 1937), licensed personal finance companies (in 1938), affiliated groups of railroad corporations (in 1938), industrial banks and Morris Plan companies (in 1942), other small loan companies and finance companies

> (in 1950), corporations renting property to shareholders for use in an active commercial, industrial or mining enterprise (in 1950, retroactive to 1945), domestic building and loan associations (in 1951), shipping enterprises depositing amounts in Merchant Marine Act reserves (in 1954), corporate affiliated groups generally (in 1954), corporations renting property to shareholders but not having other significant personal holding company income (in 1954), small business investment companies (in 1959), music publishers (in 1960), movie producers (in 1964 and again in 1976), securities dealers handling U.S. government bonds (in 1964), manufacturers leasing their products and also realizing related royalty income (in 1964 and again in 1966), corporate affiliated groups with life insurance subsidiaries (in 1974), and franchisors leasing the franchise and other property to shareholders for use in an active business (in 1976). Congress, in aiding those afflicted, has repeatedly expressed the intention to keep active businesses out of personal holding company entanglements.[1]

The same authority has also concluded: "Nonetheless, there must surely be some message from this seemingly endless parade. There is: The personal holding company tax, despite the intent of Congress, is fundamentally defective in failing adequately to shield active businesses from its impact."[2]

Another addition to this list is provided by the Tax Reform Act of 1986,[3] which modified Code §543 to exclude "active software royalties" earned by software companies from the definition of PHC income.

The 1934 regulation that included franchise royalties in the definition of PHC taxable income (the predecessor of Reg. §1.543-1(b)(3), quoted earlier) has remained virtually intact since its inception.[4] If blind adherence to the regulation was in order, the standard payments, contingent on productivity, received by franchisors and denominated royalties or license fees under most franchise agreements would clearly be PHC income.

A regulation is generally accorded a strong presumption of correctness. Even greater weight is accorded a regulation that remains undisturbed in the midst of change—congressional reapproval is implied. However, as noted above, Congress has repeatedly gone on record as being opposed to subjecting active businesses to the PHC tax.

A review of the legislative history leads one to believe that in spite of the language of Reg. §1.543-1(b)(3), it was *not* Congress's intent to have active business format franchisors subjected to the PHC tax on the franchisee-related revenues they receive, even though such revenues are denominated royalties. However, under the IRS's mechanical approach, the risk of accidental inclusion is real and the stakes are substantial.

§602 [1]Morgan, The Domestic Technology Base Company: The Dilemma of an Operating Company Which Might Be a Personal Holding Company, 33 Tax L. Rev. 241-244 (1978) (footnotes omitted). Cf. Hugh Smith, Inc. v. Commissioner, discussed *infra*, note 13.

[2]Morgan, *supra* note 1, at 244.

[3]Pub. L. No. 99-514, 99th Cong., 2d Sess. (1986 Act).

[4]Reg. §86, art. 351-2(1) (1935).

§602.3 *Case Law—Franchising*

At the heart of the problem is the difficulty courts have in characterizing the revenues earned by franchisors.

Initially, the courts wrestled with the issue whether a franchise agreement constituted a sale or a license. This issue determined the characterization of the income received from such transactions. If it was a sale, the income was capital gain. If it was a license, the income was ordinary income.

The best illustration of the courts' confusion on this issue is the series of judicial actions known as the *Dairy Queen* decisions.

The first case in the group, *Dairy Queen of Oklahoma, Inc.*,[5] involved the owner of a Dairy Queen master franchise covering Oklahoma who had entered into subfranchise agreements pursuant to which the franchisor retained the ownership of the Dairy Queen machines, provided training, and furnished the formula. The franchisor also retained the right to approve the sources from which Dairy Queen's mix was to be purchased, the locations of stores, standards of construction, supplies, and sanitary conditions and the right to audit the records of subfranchisees. Only Dairy Queen products could be sold. The contract could not be assigned without the franchisor's consent and could be terminated if any material contract provisions were violated. Lump-sum and gallonage payments were received.

The Tax Court held that the powers retained precluded characterization of the franchise agreement as a sale since there was no transfer of all substantial rights. In reversing the Tax Court decision, the Court of Appeals for the Tenth Circuit concluded that there was a sale, stressing that no time limit was placed on the use of the machine, mix, or trademark.

Each succeeding *Dairy Queen* case involved different contractual terms. Perhaps this offers some measure of explanation of the conflicts in the various federal circuit court decisions. The Tax Court consistently held, irrespective of the variations in contract terms, that all payments—lump-sum or contingent—constituted licensing (ordinary) income. The court of appeals in the various circuits held as follows:

(1) The Fourth Circuit held that capital gain treatment was appropriate for the lump-sum payments, but not for the contingent payments.[6]

(2) The Fifth Circuit held that a sale had been effected but remanded the case to the lower court to determine whether the periodic payments were part of the sale price.[7]

(3) The Eighth Circuit, in its decision, looked behind the "cold contracts" to the nonobligatory activities of the franchisor and held that the franchise contracts under consideration yielded only ordinary income.[8]

(4) The Ninth Circuit, on facts identical to those considered by the Fifth Circuit,

[5]Dairy Queen of Oklahoma, Inc. v. Commissioner, 26 T.C. 61 (1956), *rev'd*, 250 F.2d 503 (10th Cir. 1958), 58-1 U.S.T.C. ¶9155.

[6]Estate of Gowdey v. Commissioner, 307 F.2d 816 (4th Cir. 1962), 62-2 U.S.T.C. ¶9603.

[7]Moberg v. Commissioner, 305 F.2d 800 (5th Cir. 1962), 62-2 U.S.T.C. ¶9662.

[8]United States v. Wernentin, 354 F.2d 757 (8th Cir. 1966), 66-1 U.S.T.C. ¶9140.

determined that there was no transfer of sufficient rights to constitute a sale and that all payments received were ordinary income.[9]

(5) The Tenth Circuit concluded that all payments, lump-sum and contingent, were taxable as capital gain.[10]

To overcome this remarkable confusion, Congress enacted Code §1253, in the Tax Reform Act of 1969,[11] which has come to be known as the *Dairy Queen* section. Code §1253 quite effectively characterized the payments received by a franchisor in practically all situations where there are significant retained rights as income from "other than the sale of a capital asset" (i.e., ordinary income). However, in enacting Code §1253, Congress gave no consideration to the PHC issue as to whether its characterization of franchise fees as ordinary income (rather than capital gain) should have any effect on the characterization of such fees for PHC purposes.

§602.4 *Case Law—"Compensation for Services" Versus "Royalty Income"*

The case law (and perhaps the change in Reg. §1.1362-3 discussed in §603 below) in this area yields the strongest argument available on behalf of the average successful closely held franchisor—that license fees and royalties paid to franchisors are not PHC income.

Some commentators have taken the position that regardless of denomination, any payment for the licensing of trade names, patents, secret processes or formulas, goodwill, trademark, or format constitutes a royalty.[12] The support usually cited for this position is *Hugh Smith, Inc. v. Commissioner.*[13] In *Smith,* the Tax Court had under consideration a license agreement to "use and vend on bottled Coca-Cola, the trademark name of Coca-Cola, and all labels and designs pertaining thereto." The licensee was required to order syrup from the taxpayer. The Tax Court held that the price for the syrup did not reflect its true value and that the major portion of the gallonage charges was attributable to the right to use the trademark on the labels. The court held that because there was no allocation, the entire amount received represented royalties and constituted PHC income. In *Dairy Queen of Oklahoma, Inc.,*[14] the Tax Court again held that lump-sum and gallonage payments from licensing agreements were PHC income.

As part of its argument, the taxpayer in *Smith* specifically contended that the definition of royalty in the regulations (the predecessor to the current Regulations §1.543-1(b)(3)) was without foundation. However, the Tax Court rejected the taxpayer's contention, specifically stating that Congress had, in effect, registered its

[9]Moberg v. Commissioner, 320 F.2d 782 (9th Cir. 1966), 66-2 U.S.T.C. ¶9824.

[10]*Dairy Queen, supra* note 5.

[11]Pub. L. No. 91-172, 91st Cong., 2d Sess. (1969 Act).

[12]See, e.g., Campbell, Income from Franchising: Capital Gain, Ordinary Income or Personal Holding Company Income, 1 Tax Advisor 540, 547 (Sept. 1970).

[13]8 T.C. 660 (1947), *aff'd,* 173 F.2d 224 (6th Cir. 1949), 49-1 U.S.T.C. ¶9196, *cert. denied,* 337 U.S. 918.

[14]*Dairy Queen, supra* note 5.

approval of the subject regulation by reenactment of a practically identical provision of law without change.

It first appears that even a current day franchisor taxpayer is stymied. However, a close look at the facts in *Smith* indicates that extrication is possible. Hugh Smith, Inc. was a corporation wholly owned by an individual named Hugh Smith. Hugh Smith, Inc. (the corporate taxpayer in the case) entered into a franchise agreement with Coca-Cola that allowed the corporation to use Coca-Cola's trademark if Hugh Smith, Inc. purchased its syrup from Coca-Cola. Hugh Smith, Inc., was required to pay Coca-Cola $1.30 per gallon of syrup. The taxpayer/corporation entered into a subcontract arrangement with Hugh Smith individually that gave Smith all of the same rights to use the trademark that the corporation had and required that Smith buy the syrup from Hugh Smith, Inc., at $1.50 per gallon. The active conduct of selling the bottled beverage was conducted by Hugh Smith individually. Hugh Smith, Inc., collected its $.20 per gallon profit on the syrup.

This was not a case of royalties received by an "active" business format franchisor. The Tax Court held that a payment, however denominated, which is exclusively for the use of a trademark (as the Tax Court specifically found the payment in *Smith* to be) is a "royalty" for purposes of the PHC tax.

To understand the value of *Smith,* the reader must note the court's specific finding that the corporate taxpayer did nothing other than receive the $.20 per gallon profit. It was a purely passive entity in *Smith* which was held to be a PHC.

It can be argued that the more relevant aspect of the *Smith* case, with respect to its applicability to the Roman Lobe situation of our example or the situation of the usual business format franchisor, was the court's statement that "the cases, among which are *Kiesau Petroleum Corp.* and *U.S. Universal Joints Co.,* cited by Petitioner in support of its contention that the income involved was not from 'royalties,' are so clearly distinguishable on their facts as to require no further comment."[15]

Although the court felt the taxpayer in *Smith* was not within the facts or holding of *U.S. Universal Joints,* it by no means rejected or overturned its holding in the case. Therefore, it seems clear that *U.S. Universal Joints Co.* is still good law. The IRS has acquiesced in the case,[16] and accordingly it is appropriate for our review.

The issue for decision in *U.S. Universal Joints Co.* turned on payments denominated royalties in a written contract for the use of a patented invention. Although not specifically referring to "franchise" royalties, the court's reasoning—that the payments amounted to "compensation for services" as opposed to a purely "passive" patent royalty and that therefore the corporation was not a PHC—is, and should be, good law today.

In *U.S. Universal Joints Co.,* Murton and Guy, two automotive engineers, invented and patented the "universal joint." They contributed the patent to their corporation. The corporation, as the holder of the rights under the patent, entered into various license agreements with certain manufacturers allowing the licensees to manufacture and use the product under the patent. The invention, however,

[15]*Hugh Smith, Inc.,* 8 T.C. at 674 (citing Kiesau Petroleum Corp. v. Commissioner, 42 B.T.A. 69 (1940), and U.S. Universal Joints Co. v. Commissioner, 46 B.T.A. 111 (1942)).

[16]1942-1 C.B. 17.

had such potentially widespread application that the various licensees all needed and obtained the time, advice, and engineering services of Murton and Guy, the controlling shareholders of the corporation.

The court, in *U.S. Universal Joints Co.*, made specific findings of fact as follows:

> The licensees agreed to pay the petitioner a fixed percentage of the selling price of the licensed article. *The entire payment required under each written agreement was designated a "royalty" in the license. . . .* [Emphasis added.]
>
> At the time the license contracts were executed the parties orally agreed that petitioner would furnish to the licensees whatever engineering services were necessary in connection with the manufacture and sale of the joint. It was understood by all the parties that such services would be substantial because of the special engineering knowledge required to adapt the joint to varied uses. The parties were unable to reduce the agreement with regard to petitioner's services to writing because it was impossible to determine precisely how long or at what time petitioner's services would be required. When the contracts were executed it was also understood by the parties that petitioner was to be compensated for the services it would render to the licensees. *The "royalties" provided for in the contracts were intended by the contracting parties to be, in part, payment for the right to manufacture and use the patented joint and, in part, payment for the services to be rendered by the petitioner.* [Emphasis added.][17]

The court went on to make a specific finding with respect to how much the passive patent rights alone would bring. The rest of the "royalty" was held to be "compensation for services" and, to such extent, not PHC income regardless of the characterization in the contract solely as royalty.[18]

In terms of applying the reasoning of *U.S. Universal Joints* to the typical franchise agreement, however, it must be understood that such franchise agreement usually contemplates not merely the passive receipt of licensing fees but generally supervision and management services, expert guidance in the selection of lease sites, training of management and other personnel, guidance in efficient purchasing techniques and in the installation and maintenance of effective accounting records, and other related services.

If the franchise agreement specifically allocates a portion of the fees as compensation for services, and if such allocation is reasonable, the franchisor can escape PHC income classification for such fees. It is not uncommon for such fees to be based on a percentage of sales or of supplies purchased. The method of determination should not alter the result if the total amount received represents reasonable compensation.

§602.5 *Recommendations*

Returning to the example of Roman Lobe, Inc., at §602 above, what is the solution to its IRS dilemmas?

[17]*U.S. Universal Joints Co.*, 46 B.T.A. at 112-113.

[18]The court reasoned as follows:

> Because of competitive products it would not have been possible for the licensees to pay more than approximately 4 percent of net selling price for the use of the patented joint itself. The excess of the required payments over 4 percent of net selling price was intended to be the compensation for petitioner's advice and services.

Id. at 113.

Clearly, the first line of defense is to fight the characterization of its franchise royalty fee as a royalty for PHC purposes. Accordingly, special care should be given to the language of the franchise agreement. For a case of how *not* to word a franchise agreement, one should review *J.C. O'Connor v. Commissioner.*[19] In *O'Connor,* the taxpayer corporation, which derived all its income from patent licenses, contended that such income, though denominated as unallocated "royalties" in the license agreement, actually contained a substantial element of compensation for engineering services rendered to licensees by the corporation's controlling shareholders.

Note that the taxpayer in *U.S. Universal Joints Co.* sustained its burden[20] (and the taxpayer always bears the burden of proof in civil tax cases) that there was an express oral agreement entered into at the same time as the contract and that substantial, though not at the time quantifiable, services would also be rendered by the staff of the contracting licensor in exchange for a total payment denominated a royalty.

In *O'Connor,* however, the taxpayer did not sustain its burden of proof. The court noted in its findings of fact, "The agreement contained no provision respecting the Patent company [taxpayer] furnishing any engineering or other services to [the licensee corporations]."[21] After careful review of the documents, the court sounded the death knell to the taxpayer's attempt to avoid PHC status:

> The agreement contained no provisions respecting the Patent company furnishing any engineering or other personal services to General Mills. However, the Agreement contained the following provisions:
>
> *No Other Understandings.* It is understood and agreed that this written agreement cancels all previous proposals heretofore received by the respective parties prior to the execution thereof and constitutes the entire understanding and agreement between the parties hereto relating or pertaining to the subject matter hereof.[22]

The court, in finding the taxpayer in *O'Connor* to be a PHC, stood by the decision in *U.S. Universal Joints Co.,* citing it as the case that defines a royalty for purposes of the PHC tax "as a payment or interest reserved by an owner in return for permission to use the property loaned and usually payable in proportion to use."[23]

The moral is that it pays to be careful when selecting someone to draft your franchise documents since those documents may prevent you from escaping PHC tax liability.

If a loss is suffered on the characterization issue of "compensation for services," is there anything else one can do?

Several possible remedies may or may not be available depending on the particular facts and circumstances of the taxpayer. Of course, there are the PHC

[19] 16 T.C.M. 213, T.C. Memo. 1957-50.

[20] See *U.S. Universal Joints Co., supra* note 15.

[21] See *J.C. O'Connor, supra* note 19, at 217.

[22] Id. at 218.

[23] Id. at 222.

deficiency dividend procedures. However, a discussion of that topic is beyond the scope of this volume. The general avenues of attacking potential PHC tax liability focus on neutralizing the computation that determines whether PHC income constitutes more than 60 percent of adjusted ordinary gross income. This can sometimes be accomplished by generating or purchasing another source of high gross (though not necessarily high net) income that is not from any of the eight PHC sources. An additional strategy is for the franchisor to increase the number of company-owned outlets. The operating income from company-owned sites should not ordinarily be PHC income. However, it would not be the gross sales of the company-owned sites that would enter the computation. Rather, sales less cost of goods sold is the relevant figure because of the definition of adjusted gross income. Another possible remedy is to elect S status, because S corporations are specifically exempted from the PHC tax.

Perhaps dealing directly with the IRS would be in order. A franchisor with a good set of facts and a strong constitution could request a private letter ruling. Perhaps the IRS national office could be convinced to issue a revenue ruling, preferably holding that "royalties" received by franchisors do not constitute "royalties" for PHC purposes when the franchisor is required to perform substantial services as part of the consideration for the fees it receives.

The degree of services necessary to be considered substantial cannot, of course, be quantified or predicted with certainty. Obviously, the more service the franchisor provides to the franchisee, the stronger the taxpayer's position. Examples of such services are marketing campaigns, research and development services, supplying and supplementing operating manuals, supervision and inspection, arrangement of volume purchasing of merchandise, materials and supplies, joint advertising programs, and so on.

Some cautions must be sounded with respect to the possible remedies. For example, a specific allocation in the franchise agreement of certain payments as compensation for certain specific services should usually exempt such amounts from being characterized as PHC income. However, the flip side is that too strong an allocation could possibly be used by state and local authorities to support an argument that an out-of-state franchisor is "doing business" within its borders. This could make the franchisor subject to the state's jurisdiction, liable for the tax, and/or subject to any regulation by that state or locality.[24]

Furthermore, too much precision in an allocation formula might give franchisors problems in establishing damages with respect to "breakaway franchisees": Those who contend that they are not liable for payment for the "services" not received. It can leave the franchisor open to being sued by franchisees for failure to perform or provide such services adequately.

The PHC problem for closely held successful franchisors is a potential nightmare—it should not be ignored.

However, with professional diligence and proper advice and planning (in addition to a possible specific exemption granted by either Congress or the IRS), most

[24]See Chapter 7.

actively conducted business format franchisors that provide substantial services should be able to avoid the penalty of the PHC tax.

§603 S CORPORATIONS

Another area of concern arising out of the franchisor's receipts being denominated "royalties" was the potential application of Code §§1362 and 1375 to franchisors that had elected to become S corporations.

Those issues focused on whether franchise royalties (and/or license or service fees) constituted "passive investment income" within the ambit of the above-noted sections. The stakes were substantial. If net passive investment income existed, there were two different consequences that could flow from it:

(1) Such income can be subject to tax in the hands of the corporation (double taxation ordinarily avoided by election of S corporation status); and
(2) Under a separate test (although turning on the same definition) excess net passive income can result in the termination of the corporation's subchapter S election.

The Code defines the term "passive investment income" as including gross receipts derived from royalties, rents, dividends, interest, annuities, and sales or exchanges of stock or securities.[1]

The sting tax imposed at the corporate level is triggered if passive investment income of a corporation having subchapter C earnings and profits (i.e., from a time before the S election) exceeds 25 percent of gross receipts.[2] Thus, one method of avoiding the sting tax is to eliminate the corporation's earnings and profits by making a dividend distribution to its shareholders. It is highly recommended in such a situation that the corporation make a valid election on a timely filed return under Code §1368(e)(3). This will ensure that the distribution is first considered a C corporation dividend and the balance a distribution of S corporation previously taxed or current taxable income. This is, of course, contrary to the normal rules for characterization of such corporation distributions.

The termination of S status for a corporation with subchapter C earnings and profits is triggered if the corporation's passive investment income exceeds 25 percent of gross receipts for three consecutive taxable years.[3] Although there are important differences, the term "passive investment income" as used in subchapter S is similar to PHC income under Code §543. The underlying theory in both cases turns on the classic "business versus investment" distinction, which has numerous analogues in the tax law.

Before the Subchapter S Revision Act, the definition (for subchapter S purposes) of passive investment income was found in former Code §1372(e)(5). The regula-

§603 [1]Code §§1362(d)(3) and 1375(b)(3).
[2]Code §1375.
[3]Code §1362.

tions defining the term[4] made a special distinction between passive rental income and receipts from an active business where "significant services" were rendered to the lessee, the latter category not being considered rent. Several revenue rulings also focused on whether various receipts constituted "rents" in this context.[5]

In Revenue Ruling 75-349,[6] the "gross receipts" received by a motion picture distribution company were held not to be passive investment income. In the industry, these payments are often referred to as film rents. However, the ruling was careful to avoid characterizing the monies as anything but gross receipts.

In Revenue Ruling 71-407,[7] an S corporation that owned a franchise enabling it to operate a professional football team received "gross receipts" from television and radio networks for the right to broadcast various football games. In the industry these payments are often referred to as broadcast royalties. However, the ruling was careful to avoid characterizing the monies as anything but gross receipts.

In Private Letter Ruling 8328037,[8] the IRS was squarely confronted with the issue in the franchise context. Technically speaking, IRS private letter rulings are directed only to the taxpayers requesting them, are limited to the particular facts, and cannot be used or cited as precedent. Nonetheless, they are very informative. The IRS specifically cited (now former) Regulations §1.1372-4(b)(5)(v) as providing that the term "royalties" includes amounts received for the privilege of using franchises. The analysis focused on the difference between Regulations §1.1372-4(b)(5)(v), which addresses "royalties" and makes no mention of the "active versus passive" distinction, and Regulations §1.1372-4(b)(5)(vi), which addresses "rents" and specifically addresses the situation where significant services are rendered. The conclusion was as follows:

> Section 1.1372-4(b)(5)(vi) of the regulations permits the Internal Revenue Service to look behind the normal characterization of rents as passive income when the corporation is a bona fide operating company. However, with respect to the other categories of passive income, the regulations contain no provisions analogous to section 1.1372-4(b)(5)(vi), and hence receipts from those sources are treated as passive investment income regardless of whether or not significant services are rendered in connection with their payment.
>
> It is the position of the Service that while Congress had the intention by enacting the passive income limitations, of distinguishing between "active" and "passive" business in determining the eligibility for the benefits of subchapter S, this purpose was completely incorporated into the statute, and that no determination was intended to be made as to whether an electing corporation's income is "active" or "passive" beyond the tests provided in the statute. This position represents the weight of judicial authority. *Marshall v. Commissioner*, 510 F.2d 259 (10th Cir. 1975); *Zychinski v.*

[4]Former Reg. §1.1372-4(b)(5)(vi).

[5]See, e.g., Rev. Rul. 61-112, 1961-1 C.B. 399 (crop-share agreement where "material participation" was present); Rev. Rul. 64-232, 1964-2 C.B. 334 (equipment rental business, significant services performed); Rev. Rul. 65-91, 1965-1 C.B. 431 (warehousing, storage, and parking lot businesses); Rev. Rul. 65-83, 1965-1 C.B. 430 (payments for use of personal property).

[6]1975-2 C.B. 949.

[7]1971-2 C.B. 318.

[8]April 11, 1983.

Commissioner, 506 F.2d 637 (8th Cir. 1974), *cert. denied,* 421 U.S. 999 (1975); *Buhler Mortgage Co. v. Commissioner,* 51 T.C. 971 (1969), *aff'd. per curiam,* 443 F.2d 1362 (9th Cir. 1970); *Howell v. Commissioner,* 57 T.C. 546 (1972). The rationale behind this literal approach is that it promotes certainty in the application of the statute. In *Buhler Mortgage Co.* the court stated "The standard used by the Code and regulations does not permit us to look behind the normal characterizations of a corporation's receipts in order to classify them as active or passive."[9]

Thus, it seemed clear that the IRS position with respect to "royalties" was that it would apply a mechanical test and it would be neither confused nor distracted by facts.

In a very similar situation, the IRS concluded in Private Letter Ruling 8450025[10] that computer software "royalties" were PHC income regardless of how "active" the company that earned them was. This result was overturned by Congress in the 1986 Act, which amended Code §543 specifically to exclude "active business computer software royalties" from the definition of "royalties" for PHC purposes.[11]

In Private Letter Ruling 8642081,[12] the IRS was presented with an active software distributor in the S corporation context. The letter ruling analyzed three different situations turning on three different software programs but ultimately held:

(1) that the regulations under subchapter S of the Code prior to its amendment by the Subchapter S Revision Act, where not inconsistent with the new law, are still in effect; and
(2) that software royalties paid to the owner of copyright are "passive investment income" within the meaning of subchapter S of the Code.

Thus, franchisors were confronted with a very real dilemma with respect to the "passive investment income" limitations. Under subchapter S, the mere characterization of payments as royalties, in the context of a closely held business format franchisor, seemed to be enough to make such payments "passive investment income" for subchapter S purposes, according to the IRS mechanical approach.

These potential pitfalls have, however, been overcome. On April 17, 1992, the IRS proposed amendments to Regulations §§1.1362-0 and 1.1362-3 relating to the definition of passive investment income for S corporations.

As originally proposed, Proposed Regulations §1.1362-3(d)(5)(ii)(A)(2) read:

(2) *Royalties derived in the ordinary course of a trade or business.* "Royalties" does not include royalties derived in the ordinary course of a trade or business of licensing property. Royalties derived by a corporation are derived in the ordinary course of a trade or business of licensing property only if, based on all the facts and circumstances, the corporation—

(i) Created the property; or

[9]Priv. Ltr. Rul. 8328037 (Apr. 11, 1983).

[10]September 7, 1984.

[11]Pub. L. No. 99-514, 99th Cong., 2d Sess. (1986 Act), §645(a)(1)(A)-(C), adding Code §543(a)(1)(C).

[12]March 18, 1986.

> (ii) Performed significant services or incurred substantial costs with respect to the development or marketing of the property.

In paragraph 1 (above such proposal), the regulations state that in general, "'Royalties' means all royalties including . . . franchises. . . ."

However, after a comment letter from the author,[13] the regulation was changed and was finally adopted as Regulation §1.1362-2(c)(5)(ii)(2), which reads:

> (2) *Royalties derived in the ordinary course of a trade or business.* "Royalties" does not include royalties derived in the ordinary course of a trade or business of **franchising or** licensing property. Royalties derived by a corporation are derived in the ordinary course of a trade or business of **franchising or** licensing property only if, based on all the facts and circumstances, the corporation—
>
> (i) Created the property; or
>
> (ii) Performed significant services or incurred substantial costs with respect to the development or marketing of the property.

Accordingly, there no longer seems to be a problem with franchise "royalties" being deemed passive income for subchapter S purposes.

[13]With the endorsement and assistance of Samuel Starr, CPA, of Coopers & Lybrand.

7

State and Local Income Tax "Nexus"

§701 Background
§702 Due Process
§703 Commerce Clause
§704 New York
  §704.1 "Doing Business"
  §704.2 Jurisdiction
  §704.3 "Employing Capital"
  §704.4 "Allocation Formula"
§705 New Mexico
  §705.1 "Engaging in Business"
  §705.2 "Leasing Property"
§706 South Carolina
§707 Multistate Tax Commission
§708 Conclusion

§701 BACKGROUND

There is another side of the "active versus passive" distinction—the possible consequences that may flow from being deemed "active." At issue is whether the operation of a franchise by a franchisee in a particular state can be deemed a sufficient connection with that state by the franchisor to constitute a "nexus" for income tax purposes.

A foreign corporation is only subject to a state's income tax if there is a sufficient nexus between the taxing state and the foreign corporation. Herein, foreign corporation means a domestic U.S. corporation organized and existing under the laws of a state other than the taxing jurisdiction. As a general rule, states do not require a return or impose a tax if a foreign corporation does not do business in the state. The underlying prohibition against their doing so is found in the due process clauses of both the U.S. Constitution and state constitutions and in the commerce clause of the U.S. Constitution.

§702 DUE PROCESS

The U.S. Supreme Court has held that due process "requires some definite link between the state and the person, property or transaction it seeks to tax."[1] "The Due Process Clause of the Fourteenth Amendment imposes two requirements for such state taxation: a 'minimal connection' or 'nexus' between the interstate activities and the taxing state and 'a rational relationship between the income attributed to the state and the intrastate values of the enterprise.'"[2]

§703 COMMERCE CLAUSE

The broad purpose of the commerce clause is to ensure that our economic unit is the entire nation and that only the federal government has the gamut of powers necessary to control the economy, including the vital power of erecting customs barriers against foreign competition.[1] The corollary of this exclusive federal power is that the states are not separable economic units that can place themselves in a position of economic isolation.[2]

The commerce clause requires that a state tax can be applied only to an "activity with a substantial nexus within the state." In *Washington Department of Revenue v. Association of Washington Stevedoring Companies*, the Supreme Court stated: "The Court repeatedly has sustained taxes that are applied to activity with a substantial nexus with the State, that are fairly apportioned, that do not discriminate against interstate commerce, and that are fairly related to the services provided by the State."[3]

The commerce clause's substantial nexus requirement has a different purpose but is obviously similar to the due process requirement. The U.S. Supreme Court sometimes uses the clauses interchangeably to strike down the imposition of taxes.

States generally seek to tax foreign corporations that do business, employ capital, own or lease property, or maintain an office within the state.[4] Notwithstanding any state's tax statutes, however, a foreign corporation whose income is derived solely from interstate commerce cannot be taxed by a state if its activities there do not generally exceed those prescribed by Public Law 86-272, which is codified at 15 U.S.C. §§381-384.

Public Law 86-272 was enacted to overturn the U.S. Supreme Court's decision in *Northwestern States Portland Cement Co. v. Minnesota*.[5] In *Northwestern*, the U.S. Supreme Court permitted the application of a state net income tax to the income of a taxpayer engaged exclusively in interstate commerce. The Court held that such a tax satisfies the requirements of the due process clause of the U.S. Constitu-

§702 [1]Miller Bros. Co. v. Maryland, 347 U.S. 340, 344-345 (1954).
[2]Exxon Corp. v. Wisconsin Dept. of Revenue, 447 U.S. 207, 219-220 (1980).
§703 [1]H.P. Hood & Sons, Inc. v. Du Mond, 336 U.S. 525, 537-538 (1949).
[2]Id.
[3]435 U.S. 734, 750 (1978).
[4]See, e.g., New York Tax Law, ch. 60, art. 9-A, §209.1.
[5]358 U.S. 450 (1959).

tion when a corporation's activities in the taxing state are such that there is created a sufficient nexus between such activities and the tax imposed. The corporation is "sufficiently involved in local events to forge 'some definite link, some minimum connection' sufficient to satisfy due process requirement."[6]

With the explosive growth of franchising in the 1980s and 1990s, several states have shown new activity in attempts to tax foreign corporate franchisors. The issues are whether the franchisor is doing business or employing capital within a state and whether the franchisor can come within the protection of Public Law 86-272. Leasing or owning property or maintaining an office within a state is a more than sufficient nexus. Without question, it is enough to subject a foreign corporate franchisor to tax in a given jurisdiction. When these connections are absent, however, the results are less clear.

Liability for a state tax depends on the specific activities of the franchisor and the language of the taxing statute. A comparison between the undecided state of affairs in New York and the definitive pronouncements that have come from New Mexico and South Carolina serves both to highlight and to explain the issues.

§704 NEW YORK

In New York, there is an undecided state of affairs surrounding the liability for the state income tax on the specific activities of the franchisor and the applicable statutes. The relevant issues are discussed below.

§704.1 *"Doing Business"*

First, it must be noted that "doing business" is a legal term of art in three separate contexts: (1) jurisdiction, (2) tax nexus, and (3) regulatory control. New York's body of law lacks specific authority with respect to when, or if, a foreign corporate franchisor is "doing business" for purposes of the tax law. A certain amount of authority exists with respect to what constitutes doing business in the jurisdictional area involving franchisor litigants. And, as to regulatory control, the offer and sale of franchises in or from New York subjects the franchisor to certain regulatory authority of the New York Attorney General's office. There is no authority on what effect, if any, such registration by a franchisor has on the determination of whether the franchisor is "doing business" for any other purposes.

§704.2 *Jurisdiction*

The jurisdictional issue of doing business has been addressed several times. *DelBello v. Japanese Steak House, Inc.*[1] was an action to rescind a franchise contract

[6] Id. at 465.

§704 [1] 43 A.D.2d 455, 352 N.Y.S.2d 537 (1974).

and secure the refund of certain payments made by a New York franchisee. Japanese Steak House was "the franchisor of a unique restaurant idea which used a patented combination cooking and eating table in the operation of an oriental-type steak house."[2] Japanese Steak House, a Florida corporation, moved to dismiss the complaint for want of personal jurisdiction. The lower court denied the motion, but the appellate division upheld the dismissal, holding the following:

(1) that the franchise agreement did not constitute an agency relationship, and therefore, the acts of the franchisee could not be attributed to the franchisor as the actions of its agent;
(2) that in New York the independent acts by residents in a contract relationship with a foreign corporation may not be attributed to that foreign corporation; and
(3) that six acts by the franchisor, which the lower court concluded constituted the "transaction of business" in New York, were insufficient to constitute "doing business" and, therefore, did not confer jurisdiction over the franchisor.

These six acts were:

(1) advertising in the *Wall Street Journal;*
(2) negotiating by telephone with franchisees in New York;
(3) sending plans, forms, manuals, and other material to franchisees in New York in connection with the franchise;
(4) corresponding by mail with the New York State Alcoholic Control Division on behalf of franchisees;
(5) engaging in "other purposeful activities in New York State with others who had no connections with franchisees in order to further [the franchisor's] business potential within this State;"[3] and
(6) extending the above communications over a period of one year.

It is inherent in this holding, though not specifically stated, that the offer for sale by a franchisor of a franchise covering New York territory does not, of itself, constitute doing business in New York.

Sheldon Estates, Inc. v. Perkins Pancake House, Inc.[4] involved an action on an instrument for the payment of money only. Again, a foreign corporate franchisor/defendant moved for dismissal on lack of personal jurisdiction alleging that it was not doing business in New York. In this case Perkins was organized as two Ohio corporations, one the franchisor and the other the exclusive sales agent. Neither corporation had offices, telephone listings, bank accounts, or employees located in New York, and neither corporation was authorized to do business in New York.

However, James Mulcahy, a franchisee who operated a Perkins Pancake House in Binghamton, New York, was also the "Eastern representative" of Perkins Pan-

[2]Id. at 539.
[3]Id. at 352, N.Y.S.2d at 539-540.
[4]48 A.D.2d 936, 369 N.Y.S.2d 806 (1975).

cake House. Pursuant to leads supplied to him, Mulcahy contacted prospective franchisees, investigated and advised Perkins Pancake House on the feasibility of certain sites, occasionally aided in the location of sites and acted as a consultant to existing franchisees. Mulcahy was not an officer or director of Perkins Pancake House, nor did he receive any salary from it. Mulcahy's motivation was apparently the commissions and overrides he received which totaled $326.72 for the years 1968 to 1971.[5]

Because of the nature of the action (i.e., for money only, and not because of any acts by the defendant in New York State), the court found that jurisdiction could only be predicated upon the traditional "doing business" concept. This requires that the foreign corporation be engaged in a continuous and systematic course of doing business in New York to warrant a finding of "presence" in the jurisdiction. The court found that Mulcahy's acts did not demonstrate use to a degree necessary to justify a finding that Perkins Pancake House was "present" in New York for purposes of jurisdiction. Again, implicit in the court's holding is the subsumed finding that the foreign corporation's acts alone (without those of its agent, Mulcahy) did not constitute doing business or presence for jurisdictional purposes. Therefore, logically, this case also stands for the proposition that the offer and sale of franchises granting territories within the geographic confines of New York State and the operation of such franchise sites by franchisees do not alone constitute the doing of business by, or the presence of, the franchisor.

Ally & Gargano, Inc. v. Comprehensive Accounting Corp.[6] is the most recent case to have addressed this issue. Although the court found that the franchisor was "doing business" for jurisdictional purposes, it continued to pay lip service to all the general propositions that a franchisor is not doing business in New York merely by selling New York territory franchises or having New York franchisees.

Comprehensive Accounting was a Delaware corporate franchisor in the business of licensing to accountants (as franchisees) "its service name, service marks and know-how regarding the operation of an accounting practice."[7] Comprehensive Accounting had 14 of its approximately 450 franchisees operating in New York State. To sell franchises, Comprehensive Accounting advertised nationwide through various media including newspapers, magazines, direct mail solicitation, telephone solicitation, and network television commercials. Although Comprehensive Accounting employees occasionally met with potential franchisees at their places of business, those employees lacked authority to bind Comprehensive Accounting. Franchise agreements could only be accepted or executed by the Comprehensive Accounting offices in Aurora, Illinois.[8]

Prior to any formal agreement between the parties, Comprehensive Accounting representatives were in New York to attend a trade show. At that time, the representatives heard a preliminary presentation by Ally & Gargano, an advertising firm. Approximately one month later, the parties entered into an agreement, pursuant to which Ally & Gargano developed television advertisements for review and

[5] 369 N.Y.S.2d at 808.
[6] 603 F. Supp. 923 (S.D.N.Y. 1985).
[7] Id.
[8] Id. at 924.

approval by Comprehensive. In addition, certain printed advertisements were developed by Comprehensive and then sent to Ally & Gargano in New York for publication in periodicals. Occasional meetings took place in New York for the development of advertisements.

The lawsuit was brought over an alleged breach of the advertising agreement. The franchisor sought dismissal claiming want of jurisdiction. The court's discussion began with a litany of the general rules:

> N.Y.C.P.L.R. §301 provides that New York courts may exercise jurisdiction over a foreign corporation if the foreign corporation is engaged in such a continuous and systematic course of doing business in New York as to warrant a finding of its "presence" here. *Dogan v. Harbert Const. Corp.*, 507 F.Supp. 254 (S.D.N.Y. 1980); *McGowan v. Smith*, 52 N.Y.2d 268, 437 N.Y.S.2d 643, 419 N.E.2d 321 (1981). The totality of a foreign corporation's contacts with the jurisdiction must be examined to determine whether it is doing business in New York, and the decision in each case will depend on the particular facts of the case. *McIntyre v. Bakers for Democratic Union*, 54 App. Div.2d 872, 388 N.Y.S.2d 587 (1976). Mere solicitation without any other evidence of commercial activity within New York is not sufficient to establish presence. *Miller v. Surf Properties*, 4 N.Y.2d 475, 176 N.Y.S.2d 318, 151 N.E.2d 874 (1958). In addition, a plaintiff who is the agent of a defendant cannot rely on its own activities in New York to sustain a claim of jurisdiction. *Haar v. Armedoris Corp.*, 31 N.Y.2d 1040, 342 N.Y.S.2d 70, 294 N.E.2d 855 (1973). Similarly, the activities of a foreign corporation's franchises in New York cannot be relied upon to establish jurisdiction over the franchisor. *Delagi v. Volkswagenwerk Ag. of Wolfsburg*, 29 N.Y.2d 426, 328 N.Y.S.2d 653, 278 N.E.2d 895 (1972); *see also, J.E.T. Advertising Associates v. Lawn King, Inc.*, 84 App.Div.2d 744, 443 N.Y.S.2d 745 (2d Dep't 1981).[9]

The court went on to find, however:

> The facts presented in this case demonstrate that Comprehensive is doing business in New York in a manner sufficient to satisfy the requirements of §301. Comprehensive regularly solicits potential franchises and prepares advertising for existing franchises in New York. While a foreign corporation may not be held present in New York solely on the basis of its control over its New York franchises, *Delagi v. Volkswagenwerk Ag. of Wolfsberg, supra*, 328 N.Y.S. at 657, 278 N.E.2d at 897, in this case Comprehensive actively engaged in business in New York designed to service its franchisees. Its representatives travel to New York to consult with the fourteen franchisees it has in New York, and it conducts regional seminars and attends trade shows in New York. Its representatives traveled to New York to consult with Ally about and participate in the creation of advertising developed as a service to both its New York franchisees and its franchisees elsewhere. Although Ally's activities in New York as Comprehensive's agent cannot be relied upon to establish long-arm jurisdiction, Comprehensive's own activities in New York, including its visits to consult with Ally, can be considered as a factor. *See Katz Communications, Inc. v. Evening News Association*, 705 F.2d 20, 25 (2d Cir. 1983); *Adam Young, Inc. v. F&S Comm. News, Inc.*, slip op. 83 Civ. 7278 (S.D.N.Y. May 25, 1984). Because Comprehensive is engaged in both solicitation plus commercial dealings in New York on a regular basis, it is doing business in New

[9] Id. at 924-925.

York "not occasionally or casually but with a fair measure of performance and continuity." *Tauza v. Susquehanna Coal Co.*, 220 N.Y. 259, 267, 115 N.E. 915 (1917).[10]

The court implies that the action of offering and selling franchises in New York and having franchisees in New York does not alone constitute doing business in New York. This is an important threshold. Assuming such a threshold test is good law for tax purposes (which it may or may not be), the issue of doing business is really an "all facts and circumstances" test. Particular acts and contacts are to be measured on a cumulative basis. When they reach an appropriate judicial (and/or reasonable) weight, they tip the scales irrevocably into the zone of doing business, which is really an either/or test (i.e., an "all or nothing" test).

It has been suggested in certain circumstances that if the taxpayer is a Delaware corporation there is a greater likelihood that an income tax nexus will be found. It is argued that this is because the allowable allocation formulas under the Delaware income tax work very strongly against allocating income to states other than Delaware.[11]

One of the most recent pronouncements of the New York State tax authorities with respect to in-state services of foreign corporations is the case of *Construction Forms, Inc.*[12] In *Construction Forms* it was held that a foreign manufacturing corporation's provision of product distribution and technical services to New York customers through its East Coast regional manager constituted doing business in New York for corporate income tax purposes even though the corporation was not employing capital in New York, did not own or lease property in New York, and did not maintain an office in New York.

Product distribution and technical services provided by a distributor are not very dissimilar from the normal follow-up services provided by a franchisor. However, because of the protections afforded by the Federal Interstate Income Law (Public Law 86-272), the Commissioner in *Construction Forms* made a distinction between technical advice about its products given before the products were delivered and technical advice given after the products were delivered. The Commissioner held that technical advice given before product delivery was merely ancillary to the solicitation of orders and, if that were the sole activity, the taxpayer would be exempt from tax. If, however, the advice were given after the product were delivered, the activity would not be deemed solicitation of orders and the taxpayer would not be exempt from the tax.

§704.3 *"Employing Capital"*

The New York franchise (income) tax is imposed on every foreign corporation "doing business" or "employing capital" in New York.[13] The element of employing

[10]Id. at 923, 925.

[11]See State Tax Advisory Board discussing nexus, apportionment, and more during second part of Nov. 1994 meeting, 55 CCH State Tax Review No.52 (Dec. 27, 1994).

[12]TSB-A-93(8)C (New York Commissioner of Taxation and Finance, Feb. 26, 1993).

[13]New York Tax Law, ch. 60, art. 9-A, §209.1.

capital is a separately sufficient tax nexus rendering a foreign corporation liable for the New York tax whether or not it is actually doing business. Employing capital is doubly pernicious as an element because it both:

(1) yields tax liability (as an independently sufficient tax nexus); and
(2) increases tax liability (by virtue of its character as a numerator element in the allocation fraction; see the discussion at §704.4 below).

In the franchisor context, the New York State Tax Department has asserted that a franchisor's trademark is capital being used in the state.

Under a predecessor section to §209 of New York Tax Law, *People v. Kelsey*[14] was cited for the proposition that the proportionate value of a trademark employed in New York by a foreign corporation was properly treated as capital employed. However, the particular facts of the case should be noted. The Spencer Pen Company was a New Jersey corporation. Evidence showed that the corporation had an office in New York City in which it made sales and had its stock in trade, bank balances, accounts receivable, and fixtures with a fair market value of $50,000.

In 1899, when Spencer applied to New York for a license to do business as a foreign corporation, the comptroller fixed the tax based on $50,000 of capital being employed (which was the measure of the tax at that time, prior to the adoption of income taxes in 1913). Spencer paid its fee and operated under its license. The capital stock of Spencer, listed at $225,000, had originally been issued in consideration for an assignment of a trademark registered under the laws of the United States.

In 1904 the comptroller sought to raise Spencer's license fee, charging that the whole of its capital, $225,000, was being employed within the state of New York. The ultimate decision of the court denied the comptroller the right to change the license fee. However, the court held that under prior New York law, the value of the trademark was includable in determining the value of capital employed within the state.

Although the trademark belonged to a foreign corporation, it is clear that the court's finding that the trademark was valuable capital being employed in the state of New York was predicated on its finding that the foreign corporation was actively "doing business" in the state. The trademark was therefore part of the business.

Generally, for purposes of taxation, intangibles are treated as having a situs at the owner's domicile. However, intangibles may acquire a situs other than the owner's domicile if they have become an integral part of some local business of the owner. This general rule rests upon the ancient maxim (*mobilia sequuntur personam*) that movables follow the person of the owner. Therefore, when a foreign corporation secures its franchise to be a corporation outside of New York, the juristic concept follows that its person, and its intangible property, are deemed to be outside of New York State.

In *Addax Music Company, Inc.*,[15] an unreported decision of the New York State

[14] 105 App. Div. 132, 93 N.Y.S. 971, *aff'd*, 185 N.Y. 546 (1905).
[15] TSB-H-85(1)C (New York State Tax Commission, 1985).

Tax Commission that "expresses the existing audit policy of the Department of Taxation," the Tax Commission held:

> The Audit Division equated Petitioner's holding of intangible property (copyrights) and collection of royalties therefrom with "doing business" or "employing capital" in this State. It thus failed to address the crucial question, namely whether the copyrights were an integral part of some local business activity of Petitioner. . . .
>
> The test of whether a corporation is engaged in business or passively holding property has been stated as follows: "the fair test to be derived from a consideration of all of [these cases] is between a corporation which has reduced its activities to the owning and holding of property and the distribution of [what] its avails, and doing only the acts necessary to continue that status, and one which is still active and is maintaining its organization for the purpose of continued efforts in the pursuit of profit and gain, and such activities are essential to those purposes." *Von Baumbach v. Sargent Land Co.*, 242 U.S. 503, 516 (1917).

Thus, to find that an intangible is capital employed within New York State, clearly there must be two elements:

(1) the intangible; and
(2) the "doing business" in the state by the owner of the intangible.

§704.4 *"Allocation Formula"*

The New York corporate franchise tax is currently imposed at a rate of 9 percent on "allocated entire net income."[16] Entire net income is substantially the same as taxable income for federal tax purposes. The allocation formula takes into account three elements, payroll, capital and revenues, with revenues being given double weight. The following example illustrates the New York formula.

EXAMPLE

X, a successful franchisor who is doing business in New York, has gross revenues for the year of $10 million. X derives $3 million of its revenues from New York. X has legitimate deduction of $4 million and, therefore, taxable income equal to $6 million. X has no payroll in New York and employs no capital in New York. The allocation percentage is computed by determining:

(1) a payroll percentage (in this instance, 0 percent);
(2) a capital percentage (in this instance, 0 percent); and
(3) a revenue percentage (in this instance, 30 percent)

[16] 1 CCH New York Tax Reports ¶5-251.

and then adding the various percentages (with the revenue percentage included twice) and dividing the sum by four. In this case, 0% + 0% + 30% + 30% = 60%, ÷ 4 = 15%. Thus, the New York tax is: Net income ($6 million) × Tax rate (9%) = Tax due ($81,000).

In addition, if it is found that the value of X is $5 million and that one-half of such value is represented by its trademark and goodwill, that X's business in New York constitutes the employing of capital as embodied in such trademark and goodwill, and that such capital employed is deemed to be in the same percentage as revenues earned (i.e., 30 percent), then the tax due would be computed as follows: payroll percentage = 0%, capital percentage is 30% × one-half of capital-allocated intangibles = 15%; revenue percentage doubled is 30% × 2 = 60%; therefore, allocation percentage = 75% ÷ 4 = 18.75%. Thus, Net income ($6 million) × Allocation percentage (18.75%) × Tax rate (9%) = Tax Due ($101,250).

Note that having the trademark deemed the "employing of capital" in New York, on these facts, increases the franchisor's liability by approximately 25 percent on no increase in income.

The New York Department of Taxation, in an initiative that must be lauded, has "determined that an amendment to the Tax Commission's regulations delineating activities which would make a franchisor taxable in New York State is the most appropriate means of handling this issue."[17] Presumably the new regulations will provide examples and insight sufficient to apprise the franchisor community of what activities will subject them to the New York tax and what limited activities will leave them exempt.

§705 NEW MEXICO

New Mexico has a clear rule governing tax nexus. In New Mexico, the statutes and court decisions establish, beyond cavil, that a franchisor receiving license fees or royalties from a franchisee operating within New Mexico will be subject to the New Mexico gross receipts tax.

In three decisions handed down in 1979, the Court of Appeals of New Mexico upheld the taxing of foreign corporate franchisors against due process and commerce clause arguments.[1] New Mexico's highest court consistently found that the taxpayers, foreign corporate franchisors, were "engaging in business" (compare "doing business") as that term is defined in the New Mexico Gross Receipts Tax

[17]Letter from John P. Dugan, Deputy Commissioner and Counsel, New York State Department of Taxation and Finance, to Neil A. Simon, Counsel and Director of Governmental Relations, International Franchise Association, December 2, 1986.

§705 [1]Baskin-Robbins Ice Cream Co. v. Department of Taxn. and Revenue, 93 N.M. 301, 599 P.2d 1098 (Ct. App. 1979); Aamco Transmission, Inc. v. Department of Taxn. and Revenue, 93 N.M. 389, 600 P.2d 841 (Ct. App. 1979); American Dairy Queen Corp. v. Department of Taxn. and Revenue, 93 N.M. 743, 605 P.2d 251 (Ct. App. 1979).

Act. Each court's decision was based on and referred to the specific language of the statute.

§705.1 *"Engaging in Business"*

The New Mexico cases do not turn on the "all facts and circumstances" test discussed above with respect to New York in deciding the legal issue of what constitutes doing business. Rather, in New Mexico, the statutory term is "engaging in business" and the issue is strictly statutory. The court reasons as follows:

> The Director held that Creamland was engaged in business because its gross receipts were derived from leasing property in New Mexico.
>
> To determine the validity of the Director's ruling we must seek the answer in the definitional aspects of the Gross Receipts Tax Act.
>
> Section 7-9-3(E) reads:
>
> "'engaging in business' means carrying on or causing to be carried on any activity with the purpose of direct or indirect benefit;"
>
> "The definition of 'business' as stated in the statute does not say 'any *act* engaged in for gain,'but rather 'any *activity.*' Webster's New International Dictionary lists, as synonyms of *activity,* the words *occupation* and *business.* Accordingly, no definitive distinction can be drawn between the definition of *business* as used in the statute, and that of its common and accepted meaning." [Emphasis in the original.] *Novak v. Redwing,* 89 Ga.App. 755, 81 S.E.2d 222, 224 (1958). *See, State v. Spink Hutterian Brethren,* 77 S.D. 215, 90 N.W.2d 365, 379 (1959). ("The words 'occupation' and 'business' are synonyms of 'activity'.")
>
> We find that Taxpayer was "engaging in business" as defined by section 7-9-3(E). It was doing what it was organized and authorized to do. *Besser Company v. Bureau of Revenue,* 74 N.M. 377, 394 P.2d 141 (1964).[2]

In many legal and tax contexts, the issue of what comes within the definition of business is material. The characterization usually turns on the facts with respect to the particular enterprises. However, in New Mexico the court held: "[W]e find that the taxpayer was 'engaging in business' as defined by Section 7-9-3(E). It was doing what it was organized and authorized to do."[3]

Because in New York the statute seeks to assess only those who are "doing business," in terms of statutory analysis and constructions, the term "doing business" in New York law limits the taxing authority. By implication some activities within the state do not rise to the level of doing business and, therefore, the ambit of the taxing jurisdiction is limited. Only those activities that rise above a certain level under certain facts and circumstances, are taxable.

In New Mexico, on the other hand, whether a franchisor is engaging in business is not a factual issue to which the franchisor may look for exemption from tax. In the words of Judge Sutin, "Under the stringent statutory provisions of the

[2] *Baskin-Robbins, supra* note 1.

[3] *Baskin-Robbins, supra* note 1.

Gross Receipts Tax Act, no franchise can escape payment of the tax. Relief can be obtained only in the legislature, not in the Court."[4]

§705.2 *"Leasing Property"*

The New Mexico Court of Appeals has also made its position as to what constitutes "leasing property" quite clear. In *Baskin-Robbins,*[5] the taxing authority found the taxpayer engaged in business because its gross receipts were derived from "leasing property" in New Mexico. The court addressed the problem:

> The remaining issue is whether taxpayer was "leasing property employed in New Mexico" as stated in the definition of "gross receipts." Section 7-9-3(F).
>
> Section 7-9-3(J) reads:
>
> "'leasing' means *any arrangement* whereby for a consideration, *property* is employed for or by any person other than the owner of the property." [Emphasis added.]
>
> Section 7-9-3(I) reads:
>
> "'property' means . . . *licenses, franchises . . . trademarks. . . .* [Emphasis added.][6]

After referencing the statute the court went on with its analysis and concluded as follows:

> By translating the definition of "leasing" into the facts of this case, "leasing" means an Area Franchise Agreement (any arrangement) whereby for payment of royalties (a consideration) a franchise and trademark (property) are employed by Creamland [the franchisee] (any person) other than Taxpayer (owner) of the franchise and trademarks (property).
>
> When definitions of "engaging in business," "leasing" and "property" are applied to Taxpayer, Taxpayer cannot escape the fact that it is leasing property in New Mexico for which it receives royalties. The royalties are "gross receipts," the money received by Taxpayer from leasing property employed in New Mexico. Section 7-9-3(F).[7]

There is no room for an intelligent practitioner to question. Under New Mexico law, a business format franchisor with a franchise in New Mexico is subject to the gross receipts tax.

§706 SOUTH CAROLINA

By far the most talked about recent income tax nexus case to affect the franchise community is *Geoffrey, Inc. v. South Carolina Tax Commission.*[1] This has been described by one of the foremost authorities in the field as "a decision with staggering

[4] *Aamco Transmission, supra* note 1.
[5] *Baskin-Robbins, supra* note 1.
[6] *Baskin-Robbins, supra* note 1, at 1100.
[7] *Baskin-Robbins, supra* note 1, at 1101.
§706 [1] 437 S.E.2d 13 (S.C. 1993), *cert. denied.*

income tax implications."[2] In light of what has clearly been the law in New Mexico for 15 years, this author feels such hyperbole is disingenuous.

Opponents of the decision (advocates for franchisors) have condemned the decision vehemently. It has been attacked on due process grounds, on commerce clause grounds, and as being guilty of incorrect apportionment analysis. It has even been described as jeopardizing the license revenues of Walt Disney, Mickey Mouse, and Michael Jordan.[3] Is it really that bad?

Geoffrey, Inc. was a Delaware corporation. It was a wholly owned second-tier subsidiary of Toys R' Us, Inc. which was also a Delaware corporation. Geoffrey had no employees, offices, or tangible property located in South Carolina. However, Geoffrey was the owner of a number of trademarks and trade names including the Toys R' Us trade name. In 1984, Geoffrey entered into a license agreement with Toys R' Us allowing Toys R' Us to use the Toys R' Us trade name and other trademarks and trade names as well as Geoffrey's merchandising skills, techniques, and know-how in connection with the marketing promotion, advertising, and sale of products covered by the license agreement.

As compensation, Toys R' Us paid Geoffrey a royalty of 1 percent of the net sales by Toys R' Us, its affiliates, or subsidiaries. It should be noted that the trial judge in *Geoffrey* found that the rights licensed under the agreement constituted a franchise.

The South Carolina Supreme Court affirmed the trial judge's ruling that Geoffrey was subject to South Carolina income tax. The language of South Carolina Income Tax Act is the key in determining the authority of South Carolina to tax Geoffrey.

The South Carolina Income Tax Act imposes income tax upon "every foreign corporation transacting, conducting, doing business or having an income within the jurisdiction of this state," and further provides, "the term 'transacting,' 'conducting,' or 'doing business,' as used in this section, includes the engaging in or the transaction of any activity in this State for the purpose of financial profit or gain."[4]

The language of the statute is very similar to that of the New Mexico statute discussed above. The decision of the South Carolina Supreme Court is no different from that of the New Mexico court discussed above. In light of the fact that the Court of Appeals of New Mexico handed down its decisions in 1979 confirming the fact that a franchisor (by franchising in a state) had sufficient nexus for constitutional purposes and, therefore, could be taxed on its income, it is difficult for this author to understand why *Geoffrey* came as such a surprise.

Clearly a franchisor cannot raise Public Law 86-272 as a defense. A statute that provides protection only for sales of tangible personal property is irrelevant in determining whether licensing of intangibles is subject to taxation.

On a purely intellectual basis, it was interesting to see the South Carolina

[2]Hellerstein, State and Local Taxation of Intangibles Generates Increasing Controversy, 80 J. Taxn. 296 (May 1994).

[3]See Minear & Rudnick, South Carolina Extends the Reach of State Income Taxes to Franchisors, Franchise Legal Digest (Fall 1993).

[4]S.C. Code Ann. §12-7-230 (Supp. 1992).

Court's suggestion that there was sufficient nexus (other than by statute) by virtue of the "presence" of Geoffrey's intangible properties in South Carolina. This appears to be based on in rem jurisdiction—the presence of a nonresident defendant's properties in the state automatically provides a predicate for asserting jurisdiction over the nonresident. This theory is at odds with the ancient maxim *mobilia sequuntur personam,* cited above, and also was repudiated by the U.S. Supreme Court in *Shaffer v. Heitner.*[5]

In this author's opinion it is not the fact that intangibles are "located" in a state that creates tax jurisdiction but rather the specific language of the taxing statute. In the South Carolina case, the statute provides for nexus in the event of "transacting, conducting, or doing business." This is a wider net pulling in far more contacts than the definition of doing business. Court definitions of doing business exclude many transactions that are, however, not beyond the court-defined bounds of "transacting" or "conducting" business.

§707 MULTISTATE TAX COMMISSION

Many proposals regarding income tax nexus have been considered by the Multistate Tax Commission (MTC). The objective of the MTC proposals are simple: to achieve a degree of certainty so that a company can understand what the rules are and at least make a good attempt to live by them.

One of the major points of friction concerns de minimis activity. In a draft of the MTC's "statement of information," it says that "an activity conducted within a taxing state on a regular or systematic basis or pursuant to a company policy, whether such policy is in writing or not, shall not normally be considered trivial." It has been suggested that maybe where, for example, once a year a district supervisor visits customers for 10 minutes, even though such practice is regular or systematic, such minuscule contacts should not automatically be excluded from de minimis status.

In addition, the many different states (as discussed above) have their many and differing definitions of what constitutes de minimis contact for their own purposes.[1]

§708 CONCLUSION

New York, on the one hand, and New Mexico and South Carolina on the other hand, represent different parts of the spectrum of "nexus" for state and local income tax purposes. The tests and the requisite elements differ substantially in many other taxing jurisdictions and must be reviewed carefully based on the facts and circumstances of each individual situation.

[5]433 U.S. 186 (1977).

§707 [1]For a full discussion, see Advisory Board Focuses on High Court, Congress and MTC actions, 55 CCH State Tax Review No. 24 (June 13, 1994), at 16.

8

State Sales and Use Tax "Nexus"

§801 **Overview**
§802 **State Sales and Use Tax Nexus**
§803 ***National Bellas Hess, Inc. v. Illinois Department of Revenue***
§804 **Special Problems Facing the Franchise Industry**
§804.1 **Services**
§804.2 **Franchise Fees**
§805 **Taxable Components of Fees Paid Under Franchising Arrangements**
§806 **Summary**

§801 OVERVIEW

The general definition of nexus for sales and use tax purposes is the same as for income tax purposes.[1] It refers to a taxpayer's connections to a level of activity or presence within a state. However, the sales and use tax nexus is determined by using different criteria than those used in establishing a nexus for income tax purposes (as defined in Chapter 7). What are the issues pertaining to nexus for sales and use taxes for the franchise industry? How can exposure to state sales and use taxes be minimized? How is nexus determined? These are just a few of the many questions that must be considered by the franchise industry.

Currently, all states except Alaska,[2] Delaware, Montana, New Hampshire, and Oregon assess a sales tax on sales within their taxing jurisdiction for franchise companies that have sales and use tax nexus. Each state that levies a sales tax also has a parallel use tax which must be self-assessed for items consumed internally by the franchise company. The sales tax, a transactional tax, is normally not imposed until the tangible personal property has been transferred to the ultimate consumer. Current trends move toward increasing the tax base by taxing services (i.e., accounting services, legal services, and other services that had previously escaped the imposition of sales and use tax).

§801 [1]The authors wish to express particular appreciation to Russel Greenstein, CPA, of Arthur Andersen, New York, New York, for his review and additions to this chapter.

[2]Although Alaska does not impose a sales tax at the state level, there are local sales taxes imposed in certain areas.

Not all sales are subject to sales tax at the franchisor level. Sales made by franchisors to franchisees for resale purposes are exempt sales. Items sold by franchisors to the franchisee for internal consumption may be subject to the imposition of sales tax.

The state sales tax rate varies from state to state from a low of 3 percent (Colorado, North Carolina, and Wyoming) to a high of 8 percent (Connecticut). In 40 of the 45 states imposing a sales tax, the state sales tax rate ranges from 4 percent to 6 percent. The corresponding use tax is normally assessed at the same rate as the sales tax. The use tax, imposed to protect in-state businesses from unfair competition, requires the purchaser to pay a use tax on purchases from out-of-state vendors.

In addition to a state sales tax, many states allow the imposition of a local option sales tax. Currently, more than 30 states have authorized a local option tax in addition to the state sales tax. Nationally, the local option tax rate ranges between .125 percent and 5 percent.

§802 STATE SALES AND USE TAX NEXUS

What is the sales and use tax nexus and what criteria are used to determine whether such a nexus actually exists? The fundamental issue in resolving this question is whether the franchise company has sufficient activity within a state to be subject to that state's taxing jurisdiction. Failure to identify all the jurisdictions in which the franchise company has a nexus could result in substantial assessments of sales and use tax plus significant additional liabilities for penalties and interest.

The requirements that must be met to establish a nexus differ from state to state. However, these requirements can be divided into three main categories:

(1) The company has established a physical presence within the state (i.e., it maintains a business location within the state at least on a temporary basis);
(2) Sales are solicited through employees or agents working within the state (i.e., through the use of traveling salesmen, jobbers, wholesalers, and others); and
(3) The business has established an "economic presence" within the state (i.e., the company has sales from within the state through some method of solicitation that does not qualify for exemption even though the company does not have property or employees with the state).[1]

It should be noted that the "economic presence" statutes have come into severe disfavor since the U.S. Supreme Court's decision in *Quill v. North Dakota*,[2] holding that a "substantial physical presence" was still the standard for determining sales tax nexus. Many of the 36 states that enacted economic nexus statutes repealed them after *Quill*.

§802 [1]Shanley, 1990 Multistate Corporate Tax Guide 70-71 (1990).
[2]112 S. Ct. 1904 (U.S. 1992).

Until recently, the first two categories, noted above, have been the standard for determining sales and use tax nexus. However, as federal subsidies to state revenues started to decline under the Reagan administration, the need to raise additional revenues became increasingly important. Many states have now been forced to increase taxes either by increasing the tax base or by expanding the definition of nexus for income tax or sales and use tax purposes. The tax base has been expanded by increasing the items subject to sales and use tax through broader interpretations of the current statutes and regulations or through new statutes and regulations that tax previously untaxed transactions. The other method of increasing revenues, expanding the definition of what constitutes a nexus, has been effected by subjecting sales previously untaxed (due to the lack of jurisdiction) to the imposition of sales and use tax.

§803 *NATIONAL BELLAS HESS, INC. v. ILLINOIS DEPARTMENT OF REVENUE*

In 1967, the U.S. Supreme Court determined in *National Bellas Hess, Inc. v. Illinois Department of Revenue*[1] that a Missouri mail-order house that had no property or employees located in Illinois and whose only contacts with the state were through the distribution of catalogs and advertising materials could not be required to collect and remit sales and use taxes on sales placed within Illinois. The case, which continues to be cited as good law, was a clear victory for direct marketers. In effect, the U.S. Supreme Court established the criteria by which all interstate sales were judged over the past quarter of the century.

In recent years, the Multistate Tax Commission has unsuccessfully attempted to have *National Bellas Hess* overturned, and numerous states, focusing on the changes in direct marketing sales methods since 1967, have challenged the interpretation and scope of *National Bellas Hess.* However, the decision in *Quill* above has resolved the issue.

The Supreme Court has also set forth the sufficient activity requirements for establishing sales and use tax nexus in the three earlier landmark cases: *National Geographic Society v. California Board of Equalization,*[2] *General Trading Company v. Iowa State Tax Commission,*[3] and *Scripto, Inc. v. Carson.*[4] In *National Geographic,*[5] the Court found that a sufficient nexus existed for the magazine's mail-order business due to the presence of local offices (which were completely unrelated) from which advertising was solicited. The Court also found a sufficient nexus in *General Trading*[6] where the petitioner used (nonresident) traveling salespeople to conduct business in the state. Finally, in *Scripto,*[7] the Court held that using agents, jobbers,

§803 [1]386 U.S. 753 (1967).
[2]430 U.S. 551 (1977).
[3]322 U.S. 335 (1944).
[4]362 U.S. 207 (1960).
[5]430 U.S. at 556.
[6]322 U.S. at 337.
[7]362 U.S. at 211.

and wholesalers within the state to solicit on a "continuous local" basis was sufficient to establish a sales and use tax nexus.

Other cases have also had an impact on the question of a sales and use tax nexus. Since the 1940s, courts have attempted to answer the question, How much activity is sufficient to determine whether the nexus exists? *Nelson v. Sears Roebuck & Co.*,[8] decided by the U.S. Supreme Court in 1941, established the premise that maintaining in-state retail outlets is a sufficient nexus to tax the company's mail-order sales. In 1970, an Illinois court found the activities of a subsidiary constituted a sufficient nexus for the parent company in *Reader's Digest Association, Inc. v. Mahin.*[9]

Some states address the lack of voluntary registration and compliance with the sales and use tax statutes and regulations by establishing nexus teams. Currently, more than 20 states (including Illinois, Minnesota, and New York) have nexus teams. The sole purpose of the nexus team is to elicit compliance with the state's sales and use tax statutes and regulations.

In New York, there is the Revenue Opportunity Division with approximately 80 employees. Approximately 12 states have each invested $50 million in computer systems that allow them to cross-match filings using the federal ID number. In other words, if a taxpayer withholds New York State payroll taxes, the state can check the federal ID number to see whether the same company is filing income, sales/use, commercial rent, and other returns.

In addition to the individual state actions, there are five multistate compacts and several bilateral agreements between bordering states. These agreements generally require the parties to publicize the agreement, encourage voluntary registration, and exchange audit information. Potentially, the most important and far-reaching aspect of these agreements is the sharing of audit information.

The definition of nexus constantly changes. Franchisors must be aware of these changes and be prepared to challenge the state's position when necessary. In addition, franchisors must be prepared to register, collect, and remit sales and use tax when required in order to limit exposure to the taxes and to penalties and interest (which can be significant).

§804 SPECIAL PROBLEMS FACING THE FRANCHISE INDUSTRY

Franchising, like many specialized industries, has industry-specific problems and concerns. The first of these concerns, discussed below at §804.1 below, regards a recent trend in several states to enact laws imposing a sales tax on services performed for franchisees. Another issue, whether the franchise royalty fee is subject to sales tax, discussed at §804.2 below, represents another potential problem facing franchisors.

[8]312 U.S. 359, 364 (1941).

[9]44 Ill. 2d 354, 255 N.E.2d 458, 460 (1970), *cert. denied*, 399 U.S. 919.

§804.1 *Services*

The state of Connecticut has an extremely aggressive statute governing the imposition of sales tax on services performed for a franchisee. Under the Connecticut General Statutes, business services such as consulting, bookkeeping, training, and inspection are subject to a use tax. However, the statutes do allow an exemption for specific franchise fees paid for use of the franchisor's trade name.

The commonwealth of Massachusetts has amended its statutes to allow for imposition of sales tax on sales (in excess of $20,000 annually per service) to businesses that provide legal, accounting, bookkeeping, engineering, or architectural services. The actual breakdown of royalties and/or initial franchise fees may determine whether the franchisor should be collecting and remitting sales tax.

Pennsylvania, for example, taxes computer services. The Pennsylvania statute is extremely broad and would include any service performed by a franchisor for a franchisee using the computer. In addition, both Connecticut and Pennsylvania tax services based on where the benefit is received as opposed to where the service is performed or delivered.

§804.2 *Franchise Fees*

West Virginia has taken the position that franchise royalty fees are subject to a sales tax. It imposes a privilege tax upon persons engaged in business and other activities in West Virginia. The term "business," defined, includes "all activities engaged in or caused to be engaged in with the object of gain or economic benefit, either direct or indirect." The term "gross income" includes the "value proceeding or accruing from the sale of tangible personal property service."

§805 TAXABLE COMPONENTS OF FEES PAID UNDER FRANCHISING ARRANGEMENTS

Usually, the franchise fee paid by a franchisee includes some consideration for tangible personal property conveyed by the franchisor. In many states the only component of the franchise fee subject to sales and use tax is that portion attributable to the sale or exchange of tangible personal property (Connecticut also taxes certain services). The tax exposure facing a franchisor involves the valuation of the tangible personal property. When the franchise fee has not been unbundled, the franchisor may attempt to assign a "nominal" value to the tangible personal property. However, the state may require an assigned value based on the fair market value, resale price, or some other method of allocation. Consequently, the liability for sales and use taxes increases.

Franchisors should be cognizant of the current trend by numerous states to assess tax on that portion of the franchise fee allocable to the sale or exchange of tangible personal property. Once aware of this trend, the franchisor can take appropriate action to minimize the tax consequences.

§806 SUMMARY

On a national level, the trend is toward the overturn of *National Bellas Hess*.[1] The movement is supported by the National Conference of State Legislatures, the National Governors' Association, the Multistate Tax Commission, and the Federation of Tax Administrators. Congress also has legislation pending that addresses the expansion of the definition of nexus for sales and use tax purposes. It is only a matter of time until the U.S. Supreme Court is requested to review a test case attacking *National Bellas Hess*. With all this activity toward the broadening of the definition of sales and use tax nexus, the benefits afforded out-of-state franchisors under *National Bellas Hess* are in danger of becoming obsolete. Franchisors and franchisees must be aware of the potential exposure for noncompliance which includes penalties and interest, some of which may be significant.

§806 [1]National Bellas Hess, Inc. v. Illinois Department of Revenue, 386 U.S. 753 (1967).

9

International Franchising and Licensing Tax Considerations

§901 International Franchising, Generally
§902 Structuring Franchise Relationships
§902.1 "Super-Royalty" Provisions and Excise Tax ("Toll Charge") on Transfers to Foreign Entities
§903 Franchisor Directly Licenses Franchises to Unrelated Foreign Franchisees
§903.1 Treaties with the United States
§903.2 Withholding and Other Taxes Imposed on Franchise Fees
§903.3 Foreign Tax Credit
§904 Franchisor Licenses (or Sells) Franchises to Foreign Subsidiary or Other Related Party Who Sublicenses (or Licenses) to Unrelated Foreign Franchisees
§904.1 Franchise Fees Characterized as Active or Passive Income
§905 Franchisor Licenses (or Sells) Franchises Through Territorial Master Licensees Who Then Sublicense (or License) the Franchises to Foreign Franchisees Unrelated to the Franchisor or the Master Licensee
§906 Franchising Versus Licensing
§907 Planning for International Licensing and Royalty Flow
§908 Licensing and Technical Support
§909 Summary

§901 INTERNATIONAL FRANCHISING, GENERALLY

Many U.S. franchisors now franchise abroad. According to the International Franchise Association, 374 U.S. business format franchisors operated more than 35,000 outlets outside the United States during 1988.[1] In addition, U.S. product and trade

§901 [1]Franchising in the Economy, 1988-1990.

name franchises were operating in more than 160 countries in 1989, according to a study conducted by Horwath International, Stoy Hayward Franchising Services, and the IFA Educational Foundation, Inc. Many other U.S. franchisors are considering operating in foreign countries in the near future. Notwithstanding this significant expansion in the international franchising arena, entering foreign markets can be difficult. The success of these ventures depends on several factors, including the franchisor's domestic market position and its ability to adapt its system to meet foreign cultural and language differences.

§902 STRUCTURING FRANCHISE RELATIONSHIPS

When considering the tax aspects of international franchising, the overall objective in the planning process is to structure the franchise relationships in a manner that will minimize the overall effective tax (domestic and foreign) to the franchisor. Due to the complexity and interaction of the Internal Revenue Code and the varying tax statutes of each foreign country or possession, transactions that appear to be similar in nature and carry out the parties' desired objectives can result in resoundingly different tax treatment. In fact, a transaction that appears to make business sense for the franchisor may not be advisable after consideration of adverse tax consequences. We emphasize that this area of tax law is extremely complex and should be investigated thoroughly before proceeding with an international franchise arrangement.

When structuring the international franchise relationship, the franchisor has three basic structuring options:

(1) The franchisor directly franchises to unrelated foreign franchisees;
(2) The franchisor sells franchises to foreign subsidiaries or other related parties who then licenses the franchises to unrelated foreign franchisees; or
(3) The franchisor sells franchises through territorial master licensees who then license the franchises to foreign franchisees unrelated to the franchisor or the master licensee.

§902.1 "Super-Royalty" Provisions and Excise Tax ("Toll Charge") on Transfers to Foreign Entities

An analysis of the underlying tax consequences attendant to international franchise relationships must begin with an examination of the effect of entering into a contract with a franchisee in a foreign country. The franchisor must determine whether the licensing of the franchise to a foreign franchisee is, in itself, a taxable event. When property (including intangible property such as franchise rights) is transferred outside the United States to a foreign entity in an otherwise nontaxable transaction, the gain inherent in the property is subject to U.S. tax. Code §§367(d) and 482 apply "super-royalty" provisions to transfers of intangibles between related parties. In addition, Code §1491 serves as a backup provision to

Code §367; it imposes a 35 percent excise tax ("toll charge") on transfers to foreign entities not otherwise covered by Code §367(d).

The super-royalty provision of Code §482 requires recognition of income from the transfer (or license) of intangible property. Intangible property includes franchises, licenses, trademarks, trade names, or similar items.[1] Code §482 is generally applied to transfers between related parties owned or controlled by the same interests, such as a license to a subsidiary that subfranchises to unrelated foreign franchisees. The super-royalty provision requires that deemed royalty income be reallocated to U.S. sources.

A factor to be considered in such a potential reallocation of income to the United States is "the extent to which the transferee bears real risks with respect to its ability to make a profit from the intangible, or, instead, sells products produced with the intangible largely to related persons (which may involve little sales risk or activity) and has a market essentially dependent on, or assured by, such related parties' marketing efforts."[2]

Many foreign countries are members of the Organization for Economic Cooperation and Development (OECD). The OECD recognizes transfer prices based on the arm's-length method. If the IRS attempts to reallocate income to the extent it exceeds what would be an arm's-length royalty charge recognized by the OECD, foreign taxing authorities may not allow a corresponding adjustment to income of the foreign entity. In addition, the IRS may not provide for relief from foreign taxes due to the reallocation of income. In these cases, an international franchising arrangement may result in double taxation.

Because U.S. tax rates are now lower than rates in many foreign countries and U.S. foreign tax credit provisions are less liberal than their foreign counterparts, foreign tax credits may not alleviate this potential double taxation problem. Finally, foreign taxing authorities can treat these deemed royalties or foreign entity payments (super-royalties) to the U.S. parent as dividends subject to foreign withholding taxes. In addition, some countries limit the amount of royalties payable by resident affiliates to their foreign parents.

Under Code §367(d), a U.S. person transferring intangible property to a foreign corporation in a Code §351 exchange or a Code §361 reorganization is treated as having sold the property in exchange for payment that is contingent upon the productivity, use, or disposition of the intangible asset. Amounts received by the franchisor are treated as U.S.-source ordinary income even though derived from a foreign entity. This compounds the apparent problems by reducing or eliminating foreign tax credits otherwise available to the franchisor. Thus, it is imperative to structure an international franchise to a foreign related party (such as a subsidiary) as a Code §482 transaction to avoid the negative impact of the deemed change of the source of the income to domestic under Code §367(d).

As previously stated, Code §1491 imposes a 35 percent excise tax (toll charge) on transfers to foreign entities not covered by Code §367(d), but does not apply if Code §367(d) applies to the transfer of intangible property. Therefore, Code §1491 effectively provides a backup provision to Code §367, although the immedi-

§902 [1]Code §936(h)(3)(B).
[2]H.R. Rep. No. 426, 99th Cong., 2d Sess. 425 (1989).

ate excise tax is obviously more substantial. Code §482 can also apply to a transfer subject to Code §1491. This backup provision obviously could have significant detrimental impact to such arrangements.

§903 FRANCHISOR DIRECTLY LICENSES FRANCHISES TO UNRELATED FOREIGN FRANCHISEES

When a U.S. franchisor chooses to franchise directly to unrelated foreign franchisees, it must first consider the tax issues of the foreign jurisdiction and then consider the resulting U.S. tax consequences. With regard to foreign taxes, many issues must be addressed, including:

(1) foreign tax rates;
(2) the definition of income on which foreign taxes are imposed;
(3) foreign withholding provisions;
(4) sources of income under the law of the country of the franchisee;
(5) tax treaties with the United States; and
(6) other taxes, such as:

  (a) registration taxes;
  (b) customs taxes;
  (c) value-added taxes;
  (d) employee and payroll taxes; and
  (e) state, municipal, and provincial taxes.

§903.1 Treaties with the United States

Under many tax treaties, industrial and commercial profits are exempt from tax if not attributable to a permanent establishment in the franchisee's country. Therefore, if a portion of the franchise fees can be classified as industrial and commercial profits and the franchisor does not establish permanency in the foreign country, some profits would be exempt from foreign tax under such treaties. If the U.S. franchisor will not have a permanent establishment in the franchisee's country, the franchise fees should be unbundled to segregate the amounts paid for services from industrial and commercial profits. The unbundling will maximize the allocation to commercial and industrial profits versus royalties and minimize resulting foreign taxes where such tax treaties are in place. (See Chapter 2 for further explanation of potential unbundling of franchise fees.)

§903.2 Withholding and Other Taxes Imposed on Franchise Fees

Some foreign countries tax the income from a franchise operation based on a flat percentage of the gross amount received. Other countries allow the franchisor to take deductions against the income received and apply the statutory tax rates to net income. Business profits are usually taxed on a net basis at regular tax rates. Foreign withholding tax is generally not required on business profits, whereas withholding is usually required on gross royalties if they are not attributable to a business in the franchisee's country.

If a permanent establishment is not needed in a foreign franchisee's country, it is prudent to avoid inadvertently creating such an establishment because all income attributable to the permanent establishment will then be subject to the foreign country's taxes. As discussed above, business profits from a permanent establishment are generally taxed on a net basis, but income from sources outside the foreign country may be includable and the income may be taxed at significantly higher foreign tax rates. Much care and planning must be exercised to avoid this trap.

§903.3 Foreign Tax Credit

After addressing the foreign tax issues of direct international franchising, the franchisor must then consider the U.S. tax considerations. The primary consideration for U.S. taxes in conjunction with the direct foreign franchising involves the U.S. foreign tax credit for foreign taxes paid in the franchisee's country. The foreign tax credit provisions were adopted to prevent double taxation by allowing a dollar-for-dollar reduction of U.S. taxes on a U.S. taxpayer's domestic income taxes on foreign-source income.

Eligible income for the foreign tax credit must not be derived from certain foreign sources.[1] Also, the foreign tax credit is limited to the amount of foreign income taxes paid and does not apply to other types of taxes paid in the foreign country. The general limitation on foreign tax credits is computed as follows:

Foreign source taxable income / Worldwide taxable income × Total U.S. tax before credits = Maximum foreign tax credit allowed during tax year

This limitation must also be calculated on different pools of income (active income, passive income, financial services income, etc.) in a manner similar to the activity-by-activity basis now required under the passive loss limitation rules.[2] Calculation of the limitations on the various pools can substantially affect the amount of foreign tax credit allowed. The treatment of income for U.S. tax purposes will determine which pool the income falls into for foreign tax credit calculations.

If the royalties received are considered active business income, the income will be placed in the general pool. In order for the royalties to qualify as active business income, they must meet certain specific tests.[3] Royalties that are not earned in the active pursuit of a trade or business fall into either the general pool or the passive pool. This determination depends on whether the royalties are taxed at

§903 [1]Code §901(j).
[2]Code §904(d).
[3]Reg. §1.954A-2(d)(1)(iii).

rates[4] higher in the general pool or lower in the passive pool than the top U.S. tax rate.

As discussed previously, sourcing of the income can be extremely important for the foreign tax credit. The source of royalty and services income will generally be where the services are performed or where the franchise rights are used (i.e., the foreign country of the franchisee).[5] Inventory and other sales of goods are generally sourced where title to the property passes.[6] As a general rule, deductions attributable to income earned from the franchise are sourced according to the source of the income. However, there is a special apportionment rule for U.S. research expenses.[7]

Based on the general rules described above, a more favorable choice by the U.S. franchisor might be indirect franchising so as to maximize the amount of franchise income allocable to the lower-taxed pool. Royalty income is considered active if the franchisor is regularly engaged in the development and licensing of property of a similar kind or if the franchisor maintains an organization in a foreign country that is regularly involved in marketing the licensed property. In addition, the marketing organization must be substantial in relation to the royalties derived from the franchising activities.[8] Whether the organization in the foreign country is considered substantial in relation to the level of royalties derived is a factual question. However, a safe harbor is provided if the sum of the franchisor's ordinary and necessary business expenses incurred by the foreign organization equals or exceeds 25 percent of gross royalty income after certain adjustments.[9] Obviously, in order to meet the safe harbor, the U.S. franchisor would have to have a significant foreign organization, which may not be feasible or advisable from a business standpoint. For instance, a significant foreign organization may be considered a permanent establishment, and consequently the franchisor may be subject to regular tax in the foreign country. (See the earlier discussion at §903.2 above.)

If the franchise fees are for significant services or goods provided to the franchisee, the franchisor could generate lower taxed or untaxed active foreign-source income. Thus, the franchisor may be able to use significantly more foreign tax credits from its active pool. This can again require an unbundling of the services to be provided and/or goods to be sold to generate U.S. tax savings. The potential savings could be in the form of increased U.S. foreign tax credits or in the form of exemption from foreign withholding.

In addition to the favorable results obtained from reclassification of foreign income, it is also prudent to minimize deductions apportioned to the foreign franchising activities. U.S. general and administrative expenses should be apportioned as much as possible to U.S. operations. This will increase the U.S. franchi-

[4]Code §904(d)(2)(A).
[5]Code §861(a)(3) and (4).
[6]Code §865(b).
[7]Reg. §1.861-8(e)(3).
[8]Reg. §1.954A-2(d)(1)(iii).
[9]Reg. §1.954A-2(d)(1)(iii)(b)(2).

sor's foreign tax credit limitation and, consequently, allow more of the foreign tax credit to be used currently.

§904 FRANCHISOR LICENSES (OR SELLS) FRANCHISES TO FOREIGN SUBSIDIARY OR OTHER RELATED PARTY WHO SUBLICENSES (OR LICENSES) TO UNRELATED FOREIGN FRANCHISEES

"Related party on-licensing" is the term often given to the selling of franchises to a foreign subsidiary or other related party who then licenses the franchises to unrelated foreign franchisees. The primary advantages of related party on-licensing are that it allows for the accumulation of income in lower-tax countries and the repatriation of income to the United States with little or no foreign withholding. It can also allow reduced withholding on royalties if the foreign country has a more favorable treaty than does the United States with the franchisee's country. However, U.S. taxing authorities have enacted a number of rules to curb abuse of the favorable tax treaties and to tax currently the accumulation of passive income in tax havens.

In order for the franchisor to enjoy the apparent tax savings from such an on-licensing arrangement:

(1) The foreign subsidiary or other related party must be a qualified resident of a country with a favorable tax treaty with the franchisee's country that provides for no or favorable withholding rates on royalties;
(2) The franchisee's country must not recast the arrangement as if the U.S. franchisor received the payments directly and impose a higher rate of withholding;
(3) The foreign subsidiary must accumulate the income subject to little or no tax on the earnings in its country;
(4) The U.S. government must not consider the foreign subsidiary's income as Subpart F income;
(5) The foreign subsidiary must be able to repatriate the income to the U.S. with little or no withholding imposed by the foreign subsidiary's country on the payments made to the U.S. franchisor, whether they are considered royalties, dividends, etc.; and
(6) U.S. foreign tax credits must be available to the U.S. franchisor for any foreign taxes paid by the foreign subsidiary.

If any of the conditions described above are not met, the U.S. franchisor cannot achieve any tax savings through such an on-licensing arrangement and could actually incur additional taxes.

One pitfall to avoid in conjunction with an on-licensing arrangement is to have the U.S. franchisor license rather than sell or make a capital contribution of the franchise to the foreign subsidiary or other related party. A sale would trigger gain to the U.S. franchisor to the extent of all gain inherent in the franchise. Such a sale to a related corporation may be treated as a capital contribution and thus subject to Code §367(d). As described previously, such a transfer creates U.S. source income that can limit the franchisor's U.S. foreign tax credit and generate super-royalties. In most cases, these results will not be desirable. Assuming that all the tests and objectives can be met, a closer analysis of the foreign tax issues and U.S. tax considerations must be made before selecting the related party on-licensing structure of international franchising.

In analyzing the foreign tax issues, both the law of the foreign subsidiary's country and that of the franchisee's country must be reviewed in detail. The foreign subsidiary can be taxed on licensing income both in its resident country and in the country of the franchisee. It must be determined whether the foreign subsidiary's country has a treaty with the franchisee's country and whether it is more beneficial than the U.S. treaty with the franchisee's country. If so, a determination must be made whether the foreign subsidiary is a qualified resident of the country and thus entitled to the treaty benefits. Finally, a careful examination of treaty abuse provisions must be conducted. There can be some very complex issues with these arrangements when three or more countries are involved in on-licensing.

§904.1 *Franchise Fees Characterized as Active or Passive Income*

Once the taxpayer is comfortable with the foreign tax issues of the related party on-licensing arrangement, it is necessary to analyze the U.S. tax considerations. The most important issue regarding U.S. taxation of related party on-licensing arrangements is whether the income is deemed to be active or passive for U.S. purposes. Passive income will subject a U.S. franchisor to U.S. taxes.[1] Tax on active income, such as remuneration for services and business income (and possibly even royalties) earned by the foreign subsidiary or other related party, can be deferred by the U.S. franchisor.[2] In order to qualify the royalties received as active income and enjoy the benefits of U.S. tax deferral, the related party must be heavily involved in marketing the franchise or actively conducting franchising activities through a substantial foreign organization.[3]

In addition to meeting the requirements described above for type of income received, it is also imperative that the foreign related party is not a passive foreign investment company as defined under the Code.[4] There are specific tests that must be met to escape various unfavorable provisions, including interest charges on the U.S. deferred tax amount.[5]

§904 [1]Code §§954(c)(1)(A) and (a)(1) and 951(a)(1).
[2]Code §954(c)(2)(A).
[3]Reg. §1.954A-2(d)(1)(iii).
[4]Code §1296(a).
[5]Code §1291.

§905 FRANCHISOR LICENSES (OR SELLS) FRANCHISES THROUGH TERRITORIAL MASTER LICENSEES WHO THEN SUBLICENSE (OR LICENSE) THE FRANCHISES TO FOREIGN FRANCHISEES UNRELATED TO THE FRANCHISOR OR THE MASTER LICENSEE

This potential structure for international franchise relationships will require much of the same analysis described in the two previous structuring options. Generally, whether the franchisor indirectly licenses its franchises to foreign franchisees through a territorial master licensee or directly to the unrelated foreign franchisees, the consequences and analysis are usually the same for tax purposes. Obviously, the business and communications aspects of evaluating these two options may be quite different from the tax considerations. In general, the U.S. franchisor must first determine the taxability of the franchise fees collected in the franchisee's country. This analysis includes consideration for taxes other than income taxes as described earlier and the potential availability of relief under tax treaties. In addition, the U.S. franchisor again has to analyze the availability and limitations of U.S. foreign tax credits. The U.S. franchisor should also determine potential taxes on the repatriation of profits or on the liquidation of the franchise.

This chapter has not reviewed any of the aspects of inbound transfers of foreign franchises to U.S. franchisees. As can be expected, myriad U.S. and foreign tax issues would need to be addressed in detail on such transfers.

When a franchisor desires to sell its franchise in several foreign countries, issues involved can become quite complicated. However, the tax (U.S. and foreign) savings differential resulting from a thorough review of structuring options can be extremely significant. Depending on the foreign countries considered, direct licensing could be more favorable than on-licensing and vice versa. There is no substitute for a detailed review of each of the foreign country's tax laws and treaties. The overall structure can become quite complex if the U.S. franchisor elects to establish a presence or foreign subsidiaries in the foreign countries. For activities in which related party on-licensing appear to be most favorable, careful planning is necessary to identify the countries in which to locate the entities and to characterize the income in the most advantageous manner. Overall, the most favorable structuring option may include a combination of all the techniques described in this chapter.

§906 FRANCHISING VERSUS LICENSING

It is often important to carefully distinguish international franchising arrangements from international licensing. In strict legal terms, a "license" is the granting of the right to use some form of intellectual property. The intellectual property in this context is usually the trademark, trade name, service mark, know-how, or combination of these intangibles. Licensing of intellectual property rights often come with little or no ongoing interaction between licensor and licensee.

Because a business format franchise often involves the grant of the right to use the franchisor's trademarks and know-how, a franchise is itself a form of license. However, business format franchises usually extend to most aspects of an entire business format and generally involve ongoing assistance and support intended to help franchisees operate successfully. Furthermore, the franchisor in these situations normally exercises quality control measures to ensure uniformity and protect its goodwill. Thus, a franchise relationship is normally characterized by substantially greater interdependence than a licensor/licensee relationship.

Many franchisors are entering into low investment relationships on an international basis that involve teaching the licensee the basics of the business but provide little ongoing support. In fact, in many situations, support made available is offered on a fee-for-services basis only. Franchise relationships at this low interdependence end of the spectrum are generally referred to as a license, whereas those relationships with more interdependence are termed "franchise relationships."

§907 PLANNING FOR INTERNATIONAL LICENSING AND ROYALTY FLOW

As outlined earlier in this chapter, withholding taxes can represent a significant cost when a licensee resides in a nontreaty country and the country of domicile for the licensor does not grant a full credit for withholding taxes levied in nontreaty countries. The withholding tax burden can be considerably reduced or sometimes even eliminated by routing the royalty flow through a conduit company in a third country that is within the treaty network of the other two countries. Countries with extensive treaty networks are common locations for these conduit companies. The Netherlands is a notable example of a good country in which to locate a conduit. In the Netherlands, the taxing authorities provide advanced rulings within a matter of weeks as to what profit margin will be acceptable in the conduit company.

There is growing opposition to abusive tax treaties by conduit companies. This opposition has resulted in new antiabuse treaty rules in recent treaties, such as the Germany/United States and The Netherlands/United States treaties. For example, according to the "subject to tax" provision in the new Netherlands/United States treaty, treaty benefits are not allowed when the recipient is exempt from tax, because double taxation cannot then occur.

The most aggressive structuring of royalty flows arises when a licensor is situated in a tax haven country. As tax haven countries usually do not have extensive treaty networks, these structures often involve using a conduit company in a tax treaty country. The biggest threat in these situations is that the arrangement will have to face-off with legislation on controlled foreign corporations (CFCs) in the parent company's country. Under recent CFC legislation, the income of a tax haven group company can be regarded as the income of its shareholder, whether or not the income is actually distributed. The application of this CFC legislation may be avoided, however, in a number of countries when the shareholder can prove that its CFC performs a real economic function, apart from the avoidance of income tax. In addition, much substance-over-form legislation has been passed and can be used to challenge these structures. Using this legislation, the taxing authorities argued that a company has its seat where actual management and control are exercised and that the transactions must have been effected for a given purpose. With proper planning and structuring, it may still be possible to establish actual management in the tax haven.

When the tax haven company itself did not develop the intangibles, the question often arises as to how to transfer the developed intangibles to the tax haven company. As an arm's-length price must be charged for purchase of the intangibles, the transferor will usually realize a potentially significant profit that is immediately taxable. Therefore, careful planning of royalty flows must be examined but may still considerably reduce the tax burden if continuing attention is paid to the arrangement to avoid problems.

§908 LICENSING AND TECHNICAL SUPPORT

Royalties and fees for technical support services may be subject to different treatment with respect to withholding taxes. Therefore, the character of an agreement under which both a license is granted and technical support is to be provided must be closely examined. When technical support services are merely ancillary, the fees for both the services and use of the license can both be regarded and taxed as royalties and may not need to be apportioned. On the other hand, if the technical services are so important that they create a genuine mixed contract, the total remuneration for the license and these services must be apportioned on a reasonable basis and the attendant taxation consequences applied.

§909 SUMMARY

The most favorable arrangement for international franchising and/or licensing will depend on whether franchise or license fees earned are subject to tax (and the level of tax) in the franchisee's country, whether there are any tax treaties available to eliminate or reduce the foreign tax, and whether related party on-licensing can reduce the overall effective domestic and foreign taxes. Because of the complexity of these arrangements and the multitude of structuring options available in multinational franchising and licensing, compilation of a flow chart or other model is advisable for each situation under the alternatives described in order to make the decision tree easier to understand and comprehend.

10

Other Services to Franchisees and Tax Planning Considerations for the Franchisor

§1001 Tax Planning Considerations, Generally
§1002 Targeted Jobs Tax Credit Programs
§1003 Ad Valorem Tax Studies
§1004 Franchisor-Sponsored Retirement Programs for Franchise Owners
§1005 ZEESOP or ZSOP Plans
§1006 Accounting Methods and Periods
§1007 Uniform Capitalization of Inventory Costs
§1008 "Passive" Losses from Royalty Arrangements
§1009 Affiliated Company Considerations and Elections

§1001 TAX PLANNING CONSIDERATIONS, GENERALLY

In this chapter, some of the other general tax planning opportunities that are often available to franchise companies are briefly discussed. These same planning techniques can also apply to franchisees. As discussed at Chapter 2, most modern-day franchisors offer a substantial body of services to their franchisees. Properly packaged, the concepts discussed in this chapter may be offered to franchisees as additional services.

§1002 TARGETED JOBS TAX CREDIT PROGRAMS

Many franchisor and franchisee operations involve the hiring of a significant number of employees. Many franchisors fill staff positions with members of certain targeted socioeconomic groups identified by the federal government and wages paid to these employees often qualify for the federal targeted jobs tax credit.[1]

The targeted jobs tax credit officially expired on December 31, 1994, but historically Congress has extended the credit provisions retroactively for hiring individuals from one or more of the nine targeted groups. The targeted groups are:

(1) vocational rehabilitation referrals;
(2) economically disadvantaged youth, ages 18-22;
(3) economically disadvantaged Vietnam-era veterans;
(4) supplemental security income recipients;
(5) general assistance recipients;
(6) economically disadvantaged cooperative education students, ages 16-19;
(7) economically disadvantaged former convicts;
(8) recipients of aid to families with dependent children and WIN registrants; and
(9) economically disadvantaged summer youth employees, ages 16-17.[2]

The tax law previously provided for an income tax credit of 40 percent of the first $6,000 paid to these qualifying employees in the first 12 months of employment.[3] Taking advantage of this credit can help offset the effect of the loss of the investment tax credit and other tax benefits available under prior law. When a franchisor anticipates hiring targeted persons, implementation of a hiring plan to capture the necessary information will aid in taking full advantage of the tax credit opportunity.

§1003 AD VALOREM TAX STUDIES

With most retail distribution, franchisors or their franchisees often have multiple retail, storage, or warehousing locations, frequently in several states. This creates two considerations regarding ad valorem taxes. First, it may be prudent to review and consider protesting real and/or personal property tax valuations. The protest could result in lower overall property tax assessments. Because most company-owned or franchisee locations will be of standardized format and similar architecture, much leverage and efficiency can be achieved. Generally, uniform methods of valuation could be applied in these situations and valuation accepted by one state or local taxing authority can be introduced as evidence in support of a valuation for another location. Again, this process could be offered as a service to franchisees.

Second, the location of inventory and supplies could substantially affect property taxes paid. In a number of states, warehoused property is granted property tax exemption. These states offer a tax haven against the tax collectors of sur-

§1002 [1]See Code §§38(a) and (b)(2) and 51(a) and (d).
[2]Code §51(d)(1).
[3]Code §51(a) and (b).

rounding states. However, the right to exemption is hedged by conditions. Generally, the goods must be in interstate transit or marked for out-of-state delivery.

§1004 FRANCHISOR-SPONSORED RETIREMENT PROGRAMS FOR FRANCHISE OWNERS

Recently, it has become popular for franchisors to sponsor retirement programs for franchise owners. A franchisor can improve franchisee relations without investing vast amounts of capital by sponsoring a "private label" retirement plan. Private label means that the plan documents and all correspondence refer to the plan as the franchisor's specific plan. Then, to fit the desires and needs of franchisees of the system, the plan would be customized. The major provisions of a private label plan are:

(1) The franchisor is the trustee of the plan;
(2) Every participant franchisee has a separate plan;
(3) The contributions are pooled together to maximize investment opportunities for the franchisees;
(4) A limited fiduciary relationship is created to oversee the program and choose the investment options to be offered;
(5) A participation agreement is executed, limiting participation to franchisees and their employees;
(6) The limited fiduciary executes an agreement to commingle funds with the administrator and opens only one account for each investment option;
(7) Each franchisee can adopt any number of plans, make contributions whenever he or she wants, be organized as any type of business entity, have any year-end and still maintain separate plan status; and
(8) The investment pools are positioned as private label collective trust funds.

If it is custom-designed, the program establishes a service for the franchisor's most successful and established franchisees. These franchisees have access to money managers that were never available to them before. The benefits to the franchisees can be numerous and allow the franchisee (as a small business) to obtain retirement benefits and investment options normally not available.

§1005 ZEESOP OR ZSOP PLANS

As a retention tool for franchisees, some franchisors have implemented franchise security ownership plans (sometimes referred to as ZEESOP or ZSOP plans). These plans are nonqualified plans and usually involve the following general provisions:

(1) The franchisor would contribute a certain percentage of royalties, sales, or purchases in cash and/or stock. These payments would be placed into

a deferred incentive program utilizing a trust. Such programs are referred to as a ZEESOP or ZSOP (i.e., a franchise security ownership program).

(2) The contribution would be nondeductible to the franchisor and nontaxable to the franchisee at the time of contribution. Taxes would be paid on income in the fund by the franchisor during the life of the trust. Income tax deductions would be available to the franchisor at the termination of the franchise term, with the funds payable and taxable to the franchisee at the time.

(3) At the option of the franchisor, a percentage of the initial franchise fee could be contributed to the deferred ZEESOP/ZSOP as an additional incentive for the prospective franchisee to purchase the franchise.

(4) The franchisor would make a contribution at the initiation of the franchise (should a percentage of the franchise fee apply), and annually thereafter, provided stated criteria are met.

(5) The contributions to the ZEESOP/ZSOP would remain in the trust for the life of the franchisee, subject perhaps to one or more vesting schedules on a graduated basis, such as a certain vested percentage at 5 years, an additional vested percentage after 20 years, or other appropriate period relative to the duration of the franchise.

(6) The trust agreement would probably take the form of a three-party agreement between the franchisor, the franchisee, and a trustee.

(7) The trustee under the agreement would invest the assets of the trust in keeping with sound fiduciary principles based on economic conditions over the term of the agreement.

(8) Both the franchisor and the franchisee could receive current statements on a quarterly basis reporting the assets and activities of the trust.

The benefits of such a program to the franchisor and franchisees of the system generally include:

(1) an increase in the value of the franchise price;

(2) an additional incentive for the franchisee to increase sales and productivity;

(3) termination of the trust agreement and reversion of the funds to the franchisor if the franchisee terminated the franchise before the end of the franchise term;

(4) an increase in the franchisee's adherence to remaining current on receivables and on the franchise agreement in qualitative terms;

(5) the provision of a substantial estate accumulation program for the franchisee;

(6) discouraging the franchisee from terminating the franchise prior to the franchise termination date because all or a portion of the trust would be lost should that occur;

(7) an additional source of working capital to enhance net profits by selling stock of the franchisor; and

(8) "golden handcuffs"—premature termination of franchise would terminate the trust agreement and funds would revert to franchisor.

§1006 ACCOUNTING METHODS AND PERIODS

Of course, franchisors have many tax considerations not unique to the franchise industry. Start-up franchise businesses must elect their method of accounting and accounting period in their initial tax year. These decisions involve general business considerations such as seasonality of the business and the potential election of S corporation status, as well as the amount and timing for collection of initial franchise fees, royalties, or other payments. In addition to election of accounting methods and periods, franchise start-ups have several other initial tax year elections, including:

(1) election to amortize organization costs under Code §248;
(2) recurring item exception for accrual of expenses to unrelated parties under Code §461(h)(3);
(3) election to amortize start-up expenses under Code §195;
(4) ratable accrual of real property taxes election under Code §461(c);
(5) election under Code §179 to expense certain depreciable assets; and
(6) certain elections with regard to inventory methods and accounting for contracts.

§1007 UNIFORM CAPITALIZATION OF INVENTORY COSTS

Many franchise companies with gross receipts of $10 million or more are required to capitalize certain inventory costs under Code §263A. This section prescribes a uniform method for capitalization of certain inventory carrying costs. Many franchise companies are subject to these provisions, particularly if there are a number of company-owned outlets.

§1008 "PASSIVE" LOSSES FROM ROYALTY ARRANGEMENTS

As discussed at some length in Chapter 6, income derived from franchise royalties may be considered "passive" for personal holding company and S corporation purposes. Using the same logic, losses incurred from these activities can also be considered "passive" and possibly subject to significant passive loss limitations under Code §469, depending on the form in which the franchise company is doing business. Regular corporations are not generally subject to these loss limitations.

§1009 AFFILIATED COMPANY CONSIDERATIONS AND ELECTIONS

Many franchising concerns conduct their business affairs with a number of corporations in order to limit their legal liability. This is particularly common if the franchisor is actually involved in several businesses. For instance, a franchisor may include separate legal entities that are involved in businesses other than the franchising activities itself, such as equipment leasing, sale of supplies or certain proprietary products, financing activities, or real estate. In these situations, there are many affiliated company considerations and elections that must be addressed, depending on whether the entities are subsidiaries of the common parent corporation or brother/sister affiliated companies. Included in these considerations are apportionment of surtax exemptions, tax preferences, investment tax credit property limitations, and Code §179 expenses limitations. In addition, there may be many consolidated return intercompany transaction considerations.

11

Succession Planning for Franchisees

§1101 Succession Planning, Generally
§1102 Restrictions on Transfer
§1103 Permission to Transfer
§1104 Transfers to a Spouse—Overfunding the Marital Share
§1105 Valuation
§1105.1 Empirical Studies
§1105.2 Statutory Changes
§1105.3 Case Law
§1106 Potential Income Tax Liabilities
§1107 Availability of Code §6166

§1101 SUCCESSION PLANNING, GENERALLY

Franchises as ubiquitous assets have joined the list of properties with which estate and financial planners must deal. In many respects a franchise is a unique asset, and succession planning using techniques developed for other types of assets may not be viable. Sound planning requires considerable input from the franchisor as well as from the more traditional estate planners, accountants, and attorneys.

Hard-working franchisees, following the franchisor's methods religiously, can build their operation into a very successful business—what appears to be a valuable asset. However, because of the myriad restrictions customarily found in a franchise agreement, evolving a sensible estate plan for a franchise owner is far more difficult than for the old-fashioned sole proprietorship or closely held business.

Usually, the estate planner's first concern is income tax planning when the client is the proprietor of a successful business. With a franchise involved, however, prudent planners must first fix their attention on the transfer of the business itself. Most of the flexibility available to an estate planner in the privately held business context is absent. Estate planning for a franchisee requires an initial and inordinate focus on the devise or transfer itself. Only after clearing that hurdle can estate planners turn their remaining attention to the tax issues at hand.

The major issues raised when a practitioner is confronted with succession planning for a franchisee are:

(1) restrictions on the transfer of the franchise imposed by the franchise agreement;
(2) spousal transfers to take advantage of the marital deduction for estate tax purposes—these may be prohibited by the franchisor or they may cause a dramatic overfunding of the marital bequest, thereby yielding a "bunching" of assets in the spouse's estate;
(3) valuation problems (left to the preparer of the estate tax return) with respect to the "franchise," which is, effectively, a contract right for tax purposes; and
(4) miscellaneous problems such as potential income tax liabilities of the decedent for reasonable compensation or accumulated earnings tax and/or the availability of Code §6166 to defer the payment of estate taxes to take advantage of lower interest rates.

The key to any successful solution to these issues, clearly, is to plan in advance. Planning also requires obtaining the cooperation (to the best extent possible) of the franchisor because without the franchisor's consent, the best laid plans will surely go astray.

EXAMPLE

Max Landers owns four Super Duper franchises to operate fast-food stores. He is 62 years of age, has had a heart bypass operation, and is uninsurable. Landers and his wife, Roseanne, both graduated from Super D University. Therefore, they are "qualified owner-operators" within the meaning of the termination provisions of the Super Duper franchise agreement. Super Duper holds the lease on the premises as well as having contractual rights through the franchise agreement. A default or termination under the franchise agreement is grounds for termination and eviction under the lease. Landers has six children. Three of his sons and one of his daughters graduated from Super D University and are therefore qualified owner-operators. The problem: How does Landers structure an estate plan so that he leaves the greatest economic benefit of his four Super Duper stores first to his wife and the remainder to his six children, share and share alike?

§1102 RESTRICTIONS ON TRANSFER

Under the Federal Trade Commission rule and most state statutes regulating franchising, a franchise prospectus must have a section concerning renewal, termination, repurchase, modification, and assignment of the franchise. Typically, the agreements place severe restrictions on the franchisee's right to freely alienate the franchise. This area, denominated relationship/termination provisions, is often the subject of separate state legislation (sometimes in conjunction with a registration statute—and often without requiring registration). The argument that a franchisor should be obligated to show "cause" in order to terminate a franchise is very persuasive before state legislatures, although the reciprocal arguments of franchisors have ultimately been more successful. Recent legislation, and its testing in the court followed by legislative reversal in Iowa, is just one example of the laws governing this area.

The International Franchise Association in its *Franchise Opportunities Guide* cautions prospective franchisee's to look at these provisions carefully, as follows:

> Is the franchisee permitted to transfer interests in the franchise? What conditions or restrictions are placed on transfers of the franchise and of majority or minority ownership interests in the franchise? Does the franchisor have a right of first refusal with respect to proposed transfers, and if so what types of transfers does it apply to (e.g., majority ownerhsip interests or sale of business, transfers to family members or among existing owners)?

A sample provision reads as follows:

> Neither Franchisee's interest in the Franchise Agreement nor any of his rights or privileges thereunder, nor the franchised business or any interest therein, may be assigned, transferred, shared or divided, voluntarily or involuntarily, directly or indirectly, by operation of law or otherwise, in any manner, without first. . . obtaining Franchisor's approval.

This standard restriction, which franchisors impose, enables them to enforce their high-quality standards and to ensure uniformity within their system. Failure to comply with these restrictions becomes cause for termination of the agreement. Thus, a franchisee trying to go against the franchisor's demands may well end up with no franchise at all.

But the specifics of the franchise agreement must be carefully reviewed. The devil is in the details, as they say, and some of the terms may be very restrictive. Franchisees are far better off knowing about these terms before they buy than finding out about them before they sell (or die, giving rise to estate tax valuation problems)—when it is too late to plan.

Here are some specific terms:

> This Agreement and the Licensee's rights and interest hereunder shall not be subject to sale, assignment, lease or sublease, transfer or encumbrance, conveyance, consolidation, merger, (all of which are hereinafter included within the term "transfer") in whole or in part in any manner whatsoever, without the prior written consent of the Company.

That means no.

> The proposed transferee shall be interviewed at the Company's headquarters office and shall be responsible for paying all related and incidental expenses of attending such interview.

Do transferees have to bring their dental records?

> The proposed transferee or transferee's Manager shall have personally attended and satisfactorily completed the Company's initial Training Course. The transferee or transferee's Manager is responsible for paying all related and incidental expenses of attending the Training Course including, but not limited to, the cost of travel, meals, and lodging.

So, one must ask whether there are hidden expenses incidental to the transfer of a franchise. But far more important in estate/succession planning are the drop-dead details. For example,

> Notwithstanding anything herein contained to the contrary, in the event of the death or legal incapacity of the Franchisee . . . the rights and obligations of the franchisee hereunder shall inure to the benefit of such of the executors, administrators, heirs, conservators or legatees of the franchisee (collectively the "Legatee") [if he so elects within 120 days—not much time to mourn] and if the Legatee be determined by the Company, in its sole reasonable discretion, to be able to perform such duties and obligations.

Then comes the kicker, which the practitioner writing the will should be aware of:

> In the event the Company determines that the Legatee is not capable of performing all of the duties and obligations required to be performed by the franchisee under this Agreement, the Legatee *shall have 12 months from the date notice of such determination is given to transfer this Agreement to a bona fide purchaser in accordance with and subject to all of the provisions of this section.* [Emphasis added.]

Obviously, to complete a transfer of a very substantial asset, within one year of death (in a situation which, by definition, is bereft of the guiding hand who knows the ins and outs of how to run the franchise) is very difficult. Generally, it can only be done at a very substantial discount. This is particularly germane to the situation of the franchisee when the franchise(s) make up almost all of the estate. But it is do or die because the agreement goes on to say:

> If the Company determines that the proposed transferee is not capable of performing all of the duties and obligations required to be performed, fulfilled and observed by the franchisee under this Agreement or if no transfer is made by the Legatee in accordance with the terms, including time requirements, of this Section, then this Agreement shall terminate without further notice at the expiration of such twelve-month period.

Th . . . Th . . . Th . . . That's All Folks.

§1103 PERMISSION TO TRANSFER

After conducting a first meeting with the client and reviewing the relevant franchise documents, a practitioner would be well advised to contact the franchisor's legal department before going forward and devising an estate or succession plan. Otherwise, the plan may appear to do wonders for the franchisee but be unacceptable to the franchisor. Some franchisors have very definite antagonisms toward plural ownership. A father like Max Landers may be confronted with Super Duper's not allowing his six children to own the four stores collectively.

Franchisors are not cruel, belligerent blockheads; rather, they are successful business persons who learn from their mistakes. A franchisor that found that a substantial number of its operations that were owned by partners ended up in litigation between the partners causing the franchise operation to suffer (thus diminishing their royalty receipts) is loathe to condone any form of plural ownership of its franchises. Therefore, several franchisors have concluded that more than one owner will be allowed only in the husband-and-wife context—no brothers and sisters and no unrelated partners. Of course, this is not always the case. Many franchisors do allow plural ownership, or at least minority ownership (it is critical that the owner-operator maintain "control" of the franchised business).

Rarely will a franchisor prevent a sale to a qualified outsider, but frequently franchisors will not allow a devise to a partnership of working siblings. This puts the practitioner in the uncomfortable position of sometimes having to recommend a predeath sale (with none of the income tax benefits of a stepped-up basis) over a normal devise to the children.

Practitioners should be aware that most franchisors will work with the representatives of the estate of a franchisee to arrange an orderly and profitable sale if an appropriate heir is not available to be a qualified owner-operator. However, a solution can only be selected if the input of the franchisor is solicited early on in the planning. Only after consulting the franchisor will the practitioner know what can and cannot be done. This need for consultation with the franchisor cannot be emphasized too strongly. Once the specifics of the allowable succession have been defined, the practitioner can go forward with the remaining tax problems.

Because of the restrictions and time restraints on orderly transfer of a franchise, which may be the largest asset of the estate, practitioners should be aware of the use of life insurance both to provide a fund for payment of estate taxes and to provide bequests to those who will not be affiliated with the franchise after the franchisee's death.

§1104 TRANSFERS TO A SPOUSE—OVERFUNDING THE MARITAL SHARE

An effective deferral of estate tax liability can be obtained through the use of the marital deduction for transfers between spouses by Code §2056 for estate tax purposes and Code §2523 for gift tax purposes. It must be emphasized that utilization of a marital deduction is merely a deferral of estate tax and not avoidance because the amount of property transferred will eventually be taxed in the estate of the last spouse to die. Naturally, if the franchise agreement prohibits the franchise from being transferred to the spouse of the franchisee, the franchise must be sold to a third party and the proceeds transmitted to the spouse. Economic problems associated with this, however, include the probability that the franchise will be undervalued in the case of such a forced sale.

Many franchise agreements, however, are quite liberal in qualifying the surviving spouse of a deceased franchisee as the successor franchisee so that the franchise may continue in the family as a going concern. This presents the problem of bunching of assets in the estate of the surviving spouse. Under the estate and gift tax law, each taxpayer is allowed a unified credit against estate and gift tax in the amount of $192,800, subject to certain phaseouts for extremely large estates pursuant to the Revenue Act of 1987. This credit effectively allows every taxpayer to pass a total of $600,000 in value free of the estate and gift tax to *any* person. Because transfers to a spouse are only estate tax deferred, if *all* assets of a decedent are transferred to the surviving spouse, the decedent's unified credit, worth $192,800, is lost forever. In the franchise setting this presents problems when the franchise is the major asset of the estate and the surviving spouse is the only qualified successor to the franchise arrangements.

When there are insufficient assets, other than the franchise, to cover this $600,000 transfer in value, the best strategy in order to maximize the benefit of the unified credit would be to qualify a child or children of the owner-operator whenever possible as franchisees so that in the event of the franchisee's death, they could succeed to a portion of the value of the franchise at least equal to the $600,000 credit amount.

§1105 VALUATION

Code §2031 generally requires the estate tax to be imposed upon the fair market value of the estate of the deceased at the time of the deceased's death. Franchises present unique problems in the area of valuation at date of death because the franchise contract in theory terminates at the date of the franchisee's death and has no value at that time. Under this theory, the only amounts included in the gross estate of the deceased would be the value of the so-called hard assets of the franchise, including equipment, inventory, and leases. Naturally, this value is substantially less than the value of the franchise as a "going concern." Moreover, as discussed in Chapter 3, the *Canterbury* case removes the aspect of "goodwill" from the valuation formula.

In most cases, however, a franchisee's rights do not terminate at death. Franchisors are liberal concerning the sale of the franchise to a qualified third party or, in many cases, with regard to qualification of the spouse of the deceased franchisee as a successor owner-operator. But, in the situation of the sale of the franchise to a third party owner-operator, which would constitute a forced sale, the value of the franchise, in theory, would be depressed.

Thus, the valuation of a franchise for estate tax purposes must fall in some middle group between the value of the "hard" assets and the value of "going concern," depending on the restrictions on transfer and the difficulty of a transfer actually engendered by the franchise agreement. The proper valuation of a franchise, therefore, presents a unique challenge to practitioners and appraisers which should allow for some creativity. However, before resorting to a dartboard or "because I said so" methodology, a review of the recent years trend with respect to valuation cases is in order.

§1105.1 Empirical Studies

First, it should be understood that the business of valuation (i.e., appraisals) of private businesses is in its infancy, "like analysis of publicly traded stocks was in the 1960s" according to some experts.[1] Second, and most important, it must be understood that a business is worth far more if it is freely transferable. If there are restrictions on transfer, as there always are with a franchise, a proper valuation will have to include a lack of marketability discount. Moreover, if the franchise is owned by more than one person (even if related—even if husband and wife or parents and children) a discount for the minority position of such owner is also in order.

According to one study, which compared restricted stock with freely traded stock, restricted stock for smaller companies consistently sold for approximately a 35 percent discount.[2] It should be emphasized that such discounting of value is appropriate in more than one context. In the context of a valuation for estate tax purposes, these reductions work toward the desirable end of a lower estate tax due, although they also result in the distributee's receiving a lower basis for income tax purposes. However, the potential built-in gain would only be at income tax rates (approximately 32 percent on capital gain), whereas the estate tax inclusion would yield rates up to 55 percent.

If, on the other hand, the valuation is part of a divorce proceeding, or a business partition due to disaffection, the lower valuation may result in the nonowner spouse or partner feeling that such discount is inappropriate and prejudicial to their interests.

A review of the history of business valuations is in order to show why they have become so important. Although conceptual business valuations emerged in the 1920s fueled by tax legislation, their real growth took place in the 1980s. In fact, it could be said that what the Employee Retirement Income Security Act of 1974 (ERISA) did for actuaries (in the nature of a full employment act), the tax laws and court decisions of the 1980s and 1990s have done for appraisers.

As a result of the computer age and the development of many new types of securities, there has been a dramatic increase in the information available to appraisers. In addition to the computerization of stock market and financial data, there is a variety of specialty studies on other securities.[3] There are also studies

§1105 [1]Valuing a Business, Forbes, April 11, 1994, p. 98 (quoting Shannon Pratt of Willamette Management Associates).

[2]Id.

[3]See, e.g., Stocks Bonds Bills and Inflation, Ibbotson Associates, Inc., Chicago, IL (annually).

specifically focusing on lack of marketability,[4] collections of market data on the sales of small businesses,[5] and industry rules of thumb.[6]

There has also been substantial evolution in the theory of valuations. There are price/earnings and other market multiples; there are dividend discount models; and there are capital asset pricing models, debt-free approaches to valuation, discounted cash flow approaches, and option pricing models. Furthermore, analysis has focused on both control premiums and valuation discounts.[7]

§1105.2 *Statutory Changes*

Valuation has received its primary impetus as a mandated exercise from recent statutory changes and court recognition of its precepts. Some of the important law changes should be noted. In 1979, §§1104(a) and 1118 of the New York Business Corporation Law introduced minority shareholders rights. Many other states followed. Additionally, differences in valuation standards emerged, particularly the difference between fair value and fair market value.

The Deficit Reduction Act of 1984 (in retrospect a hilarious title) introduced undervaluation penalties in estate and gift tax matters.[8] The law also provided extraordinary benefits with respect to estate planning for employee stock ownership plans (ESOPs). Then the Tax Reform Act of 1986 legislated that charitable contributions of closely held stock valued at more than $10,000 required qualified appraisals.

In May 1988, the U.S. Department of Labor issued a "Proposed Regulation relating to the definition of Adequate Consideration" under ERISA which enunciated certain standards for valuing securities in ESOP transactions (after the Tax Reform Act of 1986 had eliminated the estate tax benefits given by the 1984 law). All these changes (and many others) put business valuations in the spotlight. Additionally, the Internal Revenue Service promulgated a stream of revenue rulings, technical advice memoranda, and private letter rulings.[9]

All this, coupled with the addition of chapter 14 to the Internal Revenue Code, §§2701-2704 outlining valuation rules on transfers of corporate and partnership interests, transfers of interests in trust, buy/sell agreements, and lapsing rights

[4]Emory, The Value of Marketability as Illustrated by Initial Public Offerings of Common Stock: August 1990 through January 1992, Business Valuation Review (American Society of Appraisers, December 1992). Earlier studies include periods from January 1980 to December 1991, all published by the American Society of Appraisers in Business Valuation Review.

[5]Available from the Institute of Business Appraisers, P.O. Box 1447, Boynton Beach, FL 33435.

[6]Glenn M. Desmond, Handbook of Small Business Valuation Formulas and Rules of Thumb (3rd ed., Camden, ME: Valuation Press).

[7]Houlihan, Lokey, Howard & Zukin of Los Angeles, CA, has published valuable studies in both areas. See, e.g., Using Discounts to Your Advantage: The Valuation of Fractional Interests.

[8]Code §6660.

[9]See, e.g., Rev. Rul. 81-253, 1981-2 C.B. 187 (holding that there would be no minority discounts allowable in family transactions due to family attribution), and Rev. Rul. 83-120, 1983-2 C.B. 170 (giving instruction on how to value preferred stock). In Rev. Rul. 93-12, 1993-1 C.B. 202, the IRS finally acquiesced (after many court losses) that family attribution would not prohibit minority interest discounts on transfers among family members.

or restrictions, has established the business appraising profession and given rise to its two major certifying organizations: the American Society of Appraisers and the Institute of Business Appraisers.

§1105.3 *Case Law*

As valuations have become more and more important, and looking forward to the rest of the 1990s it appears they will become even more important, there has been a dramatic increase in the awareness of valuation issues by both the courts and the Service. Courts certainly appear to have become more proactive and comfortable with making real valuation decisions rather than resorting to the Solomonic practice of splitting the difference (the *Cohan* rule, or cutting the baby in half). There has been a substantial rejection of valuations based on allegedly "comparable" companies which the courts have found to be not comparable.

The courts have also expressed a recognition for the importance of professional credentials and qualifications of business appraisers while holding that other professionals with credentials in other fields (e.g., accountants) are not necessarily accepted as knowledgeable in business valuations. Also, the IRS has increased the trained business appraisers on its staff, including many who are certified by the American Society of Appraisers or the Institute of Business Appraisers.

Some of the major business valuation court cases of the 1980s and 1990s and their main holdings are discussed below:

(1) *Estate of Bright v. United States.*[10] The court rejected family attribution and allowed minority interest discounts.

(2) *Estate of Andrews v. Commissioner.*[11] The court constructed the willing buyer-willing seller test based on a hypothetical using unrelated parties and recognized the distinction between the minority interest discount and the lack of marketability discount.

(3) *Martin v. Commissioner.*[12] The court addressed the issue of multiple-level discounts involving minority interests in a holding company that owned minority interests in other companies.

(4) *Charles W. Ward and Virginia P. Ward v. Commissioner.*[13] The court held that no discount was allowable for potential liquidation expenses at the corporate level but rejected the Service argument with respect to family attribution and allowed minority interest and lack of marketability discounts.

(5) *Northern Trust Co. v. Commissioner.*[14] The court held that the use of public companies as comparable valuation criteria was not acceptable with re-

[10] 658 F.2d 999 (5th Cir. 1981).
[11] 79 T.C. 938 (1982).
[12] 50 T.C.M. 768 (1985).
[13] 87 T.C. 78 (1986).
[14] 87 T.C. 349 (1986).

spect to a closely held company and allowed two separate discounts: 25 percent for a minority interest and 20 percent for a lack of marketability.

(6) *Estate of Saul R. Gilford.*[15] The court allowed a 33 percent discount on the value of restricted stock in a publicly traded corporation.

(7) *Estate of Stirton Oman v. Commissioner.*[16] The court held that a "key man" discount was not available because the son had taken over the operation of the business before the decedent's death.

(8) *Estate of Ralph E. Lenheim.*[17] The court allowed a 25 percent discount for minority interest and lack of marketability. Moreover, the court respected the decedent's gifts of stock to his children three months before his death as changing his interest from control to minority.

(9) *Estate of Elizabeth B. Murphy.*[18] The court held that voting and nonvoting stock should be given the same value when the holdings are enhanced by being held together. However, the court refused to accept purported transfers by the decedent just prior to her death as reducing her holdings below 50 percent.[19]

(10) *Estate of Catherine Campbell v. Commissioner.*[20] The court held, after a careful review of experts' testimony, that the taxpayer was entitled to a combined minority and lack of marketability discount of 57 percent.

(11) *Estate of Edgar V. Berg.*[21] The court held that a valuation based on *Estate of Andrews,* above, should be rejected. Moreover, and most important, however, the court assessed an undervaluation penalty under §6660 and held that an appraisal by the accountant for the business, who had previously testified as an expert in other court proceedings but was not a certified appraiser, would not be respected. This chilling holding was overturned on appeal to the Eighth Circuit, but the message is clear: An accountant will not be respected as a business appraiser solely on the basis of his expertise as an accountant.

Two other cases involving very substantial amounts of money should be noted. In *Estate of Samuel I. Newhouse v. Commissioner,*[22] the court accepted the taxpayer's experts and overturned an IRS assessment of several hundred million dollars. This case related to the Newhouse media empire and was an astounding taxpayer success.

On the other hand, the case of *Estate of Joseph H. Lauder v. Commissioner,*[23] which involved the husband of the founder of Estee Lauder, was an example of the court's rejection of a formula price in a shareholder's agreement. Nonetheless, the court allowed a 40 percent discount for lack of marketability.

[15] 88 T.C. 38 (1987).
[16] 53 T.C.M. 52 (1987).
[17] 60 T.C.M. 356 (1990).
[18] 60 T.C.M. 645 (1990).
[19] Cf. *Estate of Lenheim, supra* note 17.
[20] T.C. Memo. 1991-615.
[21] 61 T.C.M. 2949 (1991).
[22] 94 T.C. 193 (1990).
[23] T.C. Memo. 1992-736.

As these cases show, valuations must be supported by the empirical data and professional imprimatur of a certified appraiser to garner the respect of the courts. As has been noted by commentators:

> The message given by the Tax Court is clear: The failure of a taxpayer to make a cogent presentation of empirical data in arguing for discounts will most likely result in a denial of the discounts sought. Taxpayers should take notice of the admonishments of the courts to avoid unfavorable consequences.[24]

§1106 POTENTIAL INCOME TAX LIABILITIES

One potential estate planning strategy being used more and more is for business owners to employ their children in an enterprise and pay them significant salaries. This strategy has two beneficial effects:

(1) Because the entity (whether it is a C corporation, S corporation, or otherwise) obtains a deduction for these salaries, income is effectively transferred from the owner of the business to the natural objects of his bounty; and
(2) The children's salaries are free of gift tax or estate tax, and the estate of the business owner is effectively reduced.

Naturally, practitioners recommending this strategy should be mindful that compensation paid to children is often vulnerable to unreasonable compensation assertions by the IRS, which results in dividend/gift treatment in the case of a C corporation and potential income/gift characterization in the case of an S corporation. Because of this risk, the compensation paid to children should only be commensurate with their efforts in the business.

§1107 AVAILABILITY OF CODE §6166

Code §6166 provides the opportunity for an estate, which is primarily composed of assets of closely held businesses, to defer payment of the estate tax liability. The estate can defer payment of amounts attributable to the interest in a small business for a period of 15 years, with interest only being paid on the tax liability for five years. After the initial five-year period, the tax liability then retires with interest in 10 equal annual installments. This deferral can be quite beneficial when the franchise is continued as a "going concern" by the family of the franchisee because they can effectively finance a potentially large estate tax liability over a period of 15 years.

For instance, in the case of Max Landers, if his children qualified as successor owner-operators for a portion of a franchise or all his franchises after his spouse's

[24] Hall & Polacek, Strategies for Obtaining the Largest Valuation Discounts, Estate Planning, Jan./Feb. 1994, pp. 38, 44.

death and the technical requirements of Code §6166 were met, the estate tax liability could be financed over a 15-year period. The children thereby avoid having to liquidate a portion of the business to pay the estate taxes. Naturally, Code §6166 has many technical requirements for qualification. Therefore, practitioners and estate planners should be extremely careful to ensure the use of this tax deferral technique.

APPENDIX

Alternative Minimum Tax—Book Income Preferences

BACKGROUND AND LEGISLATIVE HISTORY

As part of the Tax Reform Act of 1986,[1] changes were made to the corporate alternative minimum tax. The add-on minimum tax for corporations was repealed and a 20 percent alternative minimum tax replaced it.

The old minimum tax targeted certain "preferences." The new alternative minimum tax requires certain "adjustments" to taxable income to arrive at alternative minimum taxable income. For the years 1987-1989, there is a "book income" adjustment keyed to the difference between income for tax accounting purposes and income for financial reporting purposes.

In enacting the new provision as part of the 1986 Act, the Senate Finance Committee reported:

> With respect to corporations, the committee believes that the goal of applying the minimum tax to all companies with substantial economic incomes cannot be accomplished solely by compiling a list of specific items to be treated as preferences. The minimum tax cannot successfully address concerns of both real and apparent fairness unless there is certainty that whenever a company publicly reports substantial earnings (either pursuant to public reporting requirements or through voluntary disclosure for substantial non-tax reasons), that company will pay some tax (unless it has sufficient net operating losses to offset its income for the year).
>
> Thus, the committee believes that it is important to provide that the alternative minimum taxable income of a corporation will be increased when book income for the year exceeds alternative minimum taxable income. Such a provision will increase both the real and the perceived fairness of the tax system, eliminate the highly publicized instances in which corporations with substantial book income have paid no tax, and further broaden the minimum tax base to approach economic income more closely.[2]

Appendix [1]Pub. L. No. 99-514, 99th Cong., 2d Sess. ("1986 Act").
[2]S. Rep. No. 313, 99th Cong., 2d Sess. 520 (1986).

Under the new alternative minimum tax, a corporate taxpayer must pay the greater of (1) the regular corporate tax or (2) an amount equal to 20 percent of alternative minimum taxable income (in effect, taxable income plus "preference items" or "adjustments"). For taxable years beginning in 1987, 1988 or 1989 (and those years only), alternative minimum taxable income includes one half of the amount by which "book income" exceeds taxable income. "Book income" is that which is reported on an "applicable financial statement." When there is a sufficient spread between the book income and the taxable income calculations, the alternative minimum tax is payable. This may be a wholesome result when applied to corporations playing with their books, but in the franchise context, the alternative minimum tax can be invoked to penalize innocent (and not necessarily profitable) franchisors who are caught between unusual financial reporting rules and tax accounting requirements.

Most franchisors collect an initial franchise fee from a prospective franchisee upon the execution of the franchise agreement. Generally speaking, for both cash- and accrual-method taxpayers, payments received in advance are income in the year received, provided no restriction has been placed upon their use. Note, this statement disregards the discussion of the potential planning opportunity for "unbundling" of initial franchise fees found at Chapter 3.

The IRS enforces its policy of taxing prepaid income in the year of receipt, regardless of whether the income is derived under contracts or is prepaid rent, royalties, or bonuses. Moreover, it does not matter if the period covered by the prepayment is definite or indefinite. Hence, without proper planning and supporting documentation for tax purposes, the initial franchise fee is considered income to the franchisor upon receipt.

For financial reporting purposes, however, the franchisor is obligated to treat the initial franchise fee differently. The Financial Accounting Standards Board of the American Institute of Certified Public Accountants mandates, in pertinent part:

> Franchise fee revenue from an individual franchise sale ordinarily shall be recognized, with an appropriate provision for estimated uncollectible amounts, when all material services or conditions relating to the sale have been substantially performed or satisfied by the franchisor. Substantial performance for the franchisor means that (a) the franchisor has no remaining obligation or intent—by agreement, trade practice, or law—to refund any cash received or forgive any unpaid notes or receivables; (b) substantially all of the initial services of the franchisor required by the franchise agreement have been performed; and (c) no other material conditions or obligations related to the determination of substantial performance exist. If the franchise agreement does not require the franchisor to perform initial services but a practice of voluntary rendering initial services exists or is likely to exist because of business or regulatory circumstances, substantial performance shall not be assumed until either the initial services have been substantially performed or reasonable assurance exists that the services will not be performed. The commencement of operations by the franchisee shall be presumed to be the earliest point at which substantial performance has occurred, unless it can be demonstrated that substantial performance

of all obligations including services rendered voluntarily, has occurred before that time. [Emphasis added.][3]

Accordingly, in situations where a franchisor executes a franchise agreement in one tax year but the franchise does not commence operations until the succeeding tax year, the franchisor, with no nefarious intent, has created a differential between taxable income and financial statement income. In the year of the sale no problem occurs, but in the year the franchisee commences operations, the delay may cause harsh and probably unintended results.

EXAMPLE

Franchisor X, a publicly held calendar-year taxpayer, charges a $50,000 initial franchise fee. In October 1987, X sells 10 new franchises and collects $500,000 in franchise fee revenues. X includes the $500,000 for income tax purposes in 1987, a year in which X exactly breaks even (i.e., taxable income equals zero). In the succeeding year, 1988, no new franchises are sold. Once again the company breaks even.

As a result, in 1988 franchisor X's books will show taxable income equal to zero. However, for financial reporting purposes, X will show $500,000 of income (representing the franchises sold in 1987 which were not open for operation until 1988). Hence, there is a spread between "applicable financial statement" income and taxable income. One-half of this amount is the "book income" adjustment which could result in an alternative minimum tax due for a franchisor showing zero taxable income.

This is the result mandated by IRS temporary regulations on corporate alternative minimum tax book income adjustment.[4]

The book income adjustment has been repealed. To determine corporate alternative minimum tax for post-1990 tax years, franchisors must now compute the adjusted current earnings (ACE) adjustment in lieu of the arbitrary book income adjustment which was effective for the 1987 through 1989 tax years. These new ACE provisions do not seem to have any unusual effect on franchisors or franchisees.[5]

[3]Statement of Financial Accounting Standards No. 45, Accounting for Franchise Fee Revenue.

[4]See Reg. §§1.56-0—1.56-1, proposed on April 23, 1987, and adopted on August 16, 1990, by T.D. 8307.

[5]Id.

Table of Cases

References are to sections.

Aamco Transmission, Inc. v. Department of Taxn. & Revenue, 705
Adam Young, Inc. v. F&S Comm. News, Inc., 704.2
Addax Music Co., Inc., 704.3
Akers v. Commissioner, 308
Ally & Gargano, Inc. v. Comprehensive Accounting Corp., 704.2
American Dairy Queen Corp. v. Department of Taxn. & Revenue, 705
Andrews, Est. of, v. Commissioner, 1105.3
Angelus Funeral Home v. Commissioner, 502.2, 504.1

Baskin-Robbins Ice Cream Co. v. Department of Taxn. & Revenue, 705.2
Berg, Est. of, v. Commissioner, 1105.3
Besser Co. v. Bureau of Revenue, 705.1
Broadcast Measurement Bureau, Inc. v. Commissioner, 502.1, 502.3
Bright, Est. of, v. United States, 1105.3
Buhler Mortgage Co. v. Commissioner, 603

Campbell, Est. of, v. Commissioner, 1105.3
Canterbury v. Commissioner, 306, 308, 309, 309.2.1, 309.2.2, 309.2.3, 309.3, 1105
Central Life Assurance Socy., Mutual v. Commissioner, 503.1
Construction Forms Inc., 704.2

Dairy Queen of Oklahoma, Inc. v. Commissioner, 602.3, 602.4
Delagi v. Volkswagonwerk Ag. of Wolfsburg, 704.2
DelBello v. Japanese Steak House, Inc., 704.2
Dogan v. Harbert Constr. Corp., 704.2
Dri-Power Distribs. Assn. Trust v. Commissioner, 502

Exxon Corp. v. Wisconsin Dept. of Revenue, 702

Florist's Transworld Delivery Assn. v. Commissioner, 502.4, 504, 504.1
Ford Dealers Advertising Fund Co., Inc. v. Commissioner, 502.2, 502.3,
Frank and Frieda Schochet, Trustees of Insty-Prints, Inc., National Advertising Fund Trust v. Commissioner, 502, 502.4, 503.1, 504.1, 505

Geoffrey, Inc. v. South Carolina Tax Commission, 706, 706.1
General Trading Co. v. Iowa State Tax Commission, 803
Gilford, Est. of, v. Commissioner, 1105.3
Gowdey, Est. of, v. Commissioner, 602
Greater Pittsburgh Chrysler Dealers Assn. v. Commissioner, 502.4, 502.3, 504.1

Haar v. Armedoris Corp., 704.2
Howell v. Commissioner, 603
H.P. Hood & Sons, Inc. v. Du Mond, 703
Hugh Smith, Inc. v. Commissioner, 602.4

Jefferson-Pilot Corp. v. Commissioner, 309.2.3
J.E.T. Advertising Assocs. v. Lawn King, Inc., 704.2

Katz Communications, Inc. v. Evening News Assn., 704.2
Kelsey, People v., 704.4
Kiesau Petroleum Corp. v. Commissioner, 602.4

Lenheim, Est. of, v. Commissioner, 1105

Marshall v. Commissioner, 604
Martin v. Commissioner, 1105.3
McGowan v. Smith, 704.2
McIntyre v. Bakers for Democratic Union, 704.2
Miller v. Surf Properties, 704.2
Miller Bros. Co. v. Maryland, 702
Moberg v. Commissioner, 602
Murphy, Est. of, v. Commissioner, 1105.3

National Bellas Hess, Inc. v. Illinois Dept. of Revenue, 802, 803, 806
National Geographic Socy. v. California Board of Equalization, 803
Nelson v. Sears Roebuck & Co., 803
Newhouse, Est. of, v. Commissioner, 1105.3
New York State Assn. of Real Estate Bds. Group Ins. Fund v. Commissioner, 502, 504.1
Northwestern States Portland Cement Co. v. Minnesota, 703
North Am. Oil Consolidated v. Burnet, 503.1
North Carolina Oil Jobbers Assn., Inc. v. Commissioner, 502.4
Northern Trust Co. v. Commissioner, 1105.3
Novak v. Redwing, 705.1

O'Connor v. Commissioner, 602.5
Oman, Est. of, v. Commissioner, 1105.3

Quill v. North Dakota, 802

Reader's Digest Assn., Inc. v. Mahin, 803

Scripto, Inc. v. Carson, 803
Seven-Up Co. v. Commissioner, 502, 502.1, 502.2, 502.4, 503.1
Shaffer v. Heitner, 706.1
Sheldon Estates, Inc. v. Perkins Pancake House, Inc., 704.2
Spink Hutterian Brethren, State v., 705.1
Stromstred v. Commissioner, 201

Tauza v. Susquehanna Coal Co., 704.2
Tele-Communications, Inc v. Commissioner, 309.3.2

U.S. Universal Joints Co. v. Commissioner, 602.4, 602.5

Von Baumbach v. Sargent Land Co., 704.3

Washington Dept. of Revenue v. Association of Washington Stevedoring Cos., 703
Wernentin, United States v., 602

Zorniger v. Commissioner, 308
Zychinski v. Commissioner, 603

Table of Internal Revenue Code Sections

References are to sections.

38(a) 1002
38(b)(2) 1002
51(a) 1002
51(b) 1002
51(d) 1002
51(d)(1) 1002
162 504.2
162(a) 201
179 1006, 1009
195 1006
197 301, 302, 304, 304.1.1, 304.1.2, 305, 307, 308, 402.2, 403.2, 404.2
197(d) 304.1.2
197(f) 304.1.2
197(f)(4) 304.1.2
212 304.1.2
248 1006
351 902.1
361 902.1
367 902.1
367(d) 902.1, 904
368(a)(1)(B) 107
368(a)(1)(C) 107
461(c) 1006
461(h)(3) 1006
469 1008
482 902.1
541 602.1, 603
542 602.1
543 602.2, 603
543(a)(1) 602.1
861(a)(3) 903
861(a)(4) 903
865(b) 903
901(j) 903
904(d) 903
904(d)(2)(A) 903
936(h)(3)(B) 902
951(a)(1) 904
954(a)(1) 904
954(c)(1)(A) 904
1060 6.14, 309, 309.3.3, 310, 310.1, 310.2, 310.3
1060(c) 310.3
1253 6.5, 201, 301, 302, 303, 305, 307, 308, 309, 309.3, 310.1, 310.2, 402.2, 404.2, 602.3
1253(a) 201
1253(b)(1) 301
1253(b)(2) 301
1253(b)(3) 301
1253(d) 308, 403.2, 405.2
1253(d)(1) 201, 303, 304, 306
1253(d)(1)(A) 304
1253(d)(1)(B) 304
1253(d)(2) 201, 304.1.2
1253(d)(2)(A) 304.1.1, 309, 309.3.3
1253(d)(2)(B) 304, 304.1.1, 403.2
1253(d)(3) 304.1.2
1253(d)(3)(B) 304.1.1
1291 904
1296(a) 904
1362 603
1362(d)(3) 601, 603
1368(e)(3) 603
1372(e)(5) 603
1375 603
1375(b)(3) 603
1491 902.1
2201 1105.2
2202 1105.2
2203 1105.2
2204 1105.2
6166 1107
6660 1105.3

Table of Treasury Regulations

References are to sections.

TREASURY REGULATIONS

1.56-0	Appendix
1.56-1	Appendix
1.541-1	601
1.543-1(b)(3)	602.1, 602.2, 602.4
1.861-8(e)(3)	903
1.954A-2(d)(1)(iii)	903, 904
1.954A-2(d)(1)(iii)(b)(2)	903
1.1167(a)-3	308
1.1362-0	603
1.1362-2(c)(5)(ii)(2)	603
1.1362-2(c)(5)(ii)(2)(i)	603
1.1362-2(c)(5)(ii)(2)(ii)	603
1.1362-3	602.4, 603
1.1372-4(b)(5)(v)	603
1.1372-4(b)(5)(vi)	603
86.351-2(1)	602

TEMPORARY REGULATIONS

1.197-1T	304
1.1060-1T(b)	310.3
1.1060-1T(b)(1)	304, 308, 310.3
1.1060-1T(d)	310.2
1.1060-1T(d)(2)(ii)	308
1.1060-1T(d)(2)(iii)	308

PROPOSED REGULATIONS

1.461-4	504
1.1253-1(b)	302
1.1253-1(c)(2)	201
1.1253-1(c)(3)(ii)	201
1.1253-1(d)(1)	202, 307

Table of Treasury Rulings

References are to sections.

REVENUE PROCEDURES

71-21	303.1, 307, 310.2, 506
88-24	206, 306, 308, 309.3.2
93-12	1105

REVENUE RULINGS

61-122	603
64-232	603
65-83	603
65-91	603
71-407	603
74-318	502.3
74-319	502.3
75-349	603
81-253	1105
83-120	1105

PRIVATE LETTER RULINGS

8328037	603
8450025	603
8630002	308
8642081	603
8735082	308
8735083	308

GENERAL COUNSEL MEMORANDUM

39539	308

Table of Miscellaneous Rulings

References are to sections.

FEDERAL

Deficit Reduction Act of 1984 1105.2
Tax Reform Act of 1986 1105

STATE

California Regulation and Disclosure Act, §31000 *et seq.* 5
New York Tax Law §209 703
New York Business Corporation Law §§1104(a), 1118 1105.2
S.C. Code Ann. §12-7-230 706

Table of Secondary Authorities

Advisory Board Focuses on High Court, Congress and MTC Actions, 55 CCH State Tax Review No. 24 (June 13, 1994), at 16.

Campbell, Income from Franchising: Capital Gain, Ordinary Income or Personal Holding Company Income, 1 Tax Advisor 540, 547 (Sept. 1970).

Desmond, Handbook of Small Business Valuation Formulas and Rules of Thumb (3rd ed.). Camden, ME: Valuation Press.

Emory, The Value of Marketability as Illustrated by Initial Public Offerings of Common Stock: August 1990 through January 1992, Business Valuation Review (American Society of Appraisers, Dec. 1992).

Ginsburg & Levin, Mergers, Acquisitions and Buyouts: Transactional Analysis (The Little, Brown Tax Practice Series Jan. 1995).

Hail & Polacek, Strategies for Obtaining the Largest Valuation Discounts, Estate Planning, Jan./Feb. 1994, p.38.

Hardy, Franchise Primer, Forbes, Aug. 15, 1994, p.141.

Hellerstein, State and Local Taxation of Intangibles Generates Increasing Controversy, 80 J. Taxn. 296 (May 1994).

Houlihan, Lokey, Howard, & Zukin, Using Discounts to Your Advantage: The Valuation of Fractional Interests. Los Angeles, CA.

James, Federal Income Tax Issues in Franchise Advertising Programs, 2 Franchising (ABA) 7 (Spring 1982).

Lowell, Franchise Legal Digest.

Minear & Rudnick, South Carolina Extends the Reach of State Income Taxes to Franchisors, Franchise Legal Digest (Fall 1993).

Morgan, The Domestic Technology Base Company: The Dilemma of an Operating Company Which Might Be a Personal Holding Company.

The 1989 State of Small Business: A Report of the President (U.S. Government Printing Office).

Osteryoung, Hodges, & Wells, A Valuation Model for Franchise Contracts, Business Valuation Review, June 1993, p.61.

Report of House Committee on Small Business, Franchising in the U.S. Economy: Prospects and Problems (Aug. 13, 1990).

Schaeffer, Franchise Fee Collection: Reaping the Benefit of Franchise Tax Deductions, 4 Franchise Legal Dig. 3 (1985).

Shanley, 1990 Multistate Corporate Tax Guide 70-71 (1990) Stocks Bonds Bills and Inflation. Chicago, IL: Ibbotson Associates, Inc.

U.S. Department of Commerce, Franchising in the Economy, 1986-1988, 11.

Valuing a Business, Forbes, April 11, 1994, p.98.

The Wall Street Journal, February 28, 1995, p.B2

Index

References are to sections.

Accounting methods and periods
  financial accounting. *See* Financial accounting
  generally, 1006
  tax accounting. *See* Tax accounting
Ad valorem tax studies, 1003
Advertising funds
  alternative defense, 506
  generally, 207, 507
  IRS position
    continued litigation, 502.4
    Ford Dealers Advertising Fund Co., 502.2
    generally, 502
    Insty-Prints, 502.4
    nonacquiescence, 502.3
    Seven-up Company, 502.1
  payments to fund
    deductibility, 504.2
    generally, 504
    income, 504.1
  planning considerations, 505
  purpose, 501
  tax status
    generally, 503
    separate taxpayer, fund as, 503.2
    type of entity, 503.1
Affiliated company
  considerations and elections, 1009
Area development agreements
  multiple-unit transactions. *See* Multiple-unit transactions
Area representative agreements
  multiple-unit transactions. *See* Multiple-unit transactions

Brokers
  multiple-unit transactions. *See* Multiple-unit transactions
Business format franchises, 101

Canterbury vs. Commissioner
  generally, 309.1
  going concern value
    generally, 309.2
    normal franchise context, in, 309.2.2
  good will
    generally, 309.2
    normal business context, in, 309.2.1
    normal franchise context, in, 309.2.2
  IRS arguments, 309.3, 309.3.1, 309.3.2, 309.3.3
  McDonald's facts, unique, 309.2.3
Capitalization
  uniform capitalization of inventory costs, 1007
Commerce clause, 703

Development schedules, 206.2

Fees
  amortizable franchise fee, 304.1.2
  initial franchise fees
    deductibility of franchise costs by franchises, 304.2, 304.1.1, 304.1.2
    generally, 202
    intangibles, 202.1
    protection radius, 202.1
    site selection and approval, 202.2
    transfers, 303.2
    unbundling of, 307
  license fees, 203, 303.3
  master license fees, 303.4
  service fees, 203, 303.3
  state sales and use tax "nexus", 804.2
  transfer fees
    generally, 205
    subsequent transfer fees, 303.5, 304.4
Financial accounting
  area development agreements, 403.3
  area representative agreements, 404.3
  brokers, 405.3
  subfranchising arrangements, 402.3
Ford Dealers Advertising Fund Co., 502.2
Foreign corporation
  defined, 701

Franchising (generally)
  arrangements, 201
  business format franchises, 101
  economics, 103
  history and development, 102
  international. *See* International franchising and licensing
  1990s, in the, 104
  product and trade name franchises, 101
  services, 204

Income tax
  state and local income tax nexus. *See* State and local income tax nexus
Insty-Prints, 502.4
International franchising and licensing
  excise tax (toll-charge) on transfers to foreign entities, 902.1
  franchising vs. licensing, 906
  franchisor directly franchises to unrelated foreign franchises
    foreign tax credit, 903.3
    generally, 903
    treaties with U.S., 903.1
    withholding tax, 903.2
  generally, 105, 901, 909
  licensing and royalty flow, planning for international, 907
  licensing and technical support, 908
  sale through territorial master licensees, 905
  sale to foreign subsidiary, 904
  structuring relationships, 902
  super-royalty provision on transfers to foreign entities, 902.1
  technical support and licensing, 908

Master licensees
  development schedules, 206.2
  fees
    characterization and recognition of receipts by franchisor, 303.4
    deductibility of franchise costs by franchises, 304.3
  generally, 206
  sale through territorial, 905
  territorial agreements, 206.1
Mergers and acquisitions, 107
Multiple-unit transactions
  area development agreements
    financial accounting, 403.3
    generally, 403
    legal and regulatory aspects, 403.1
    tax accounting, 403.2
  area representative agreements
    financial accounting, 404.3
    generally, 404
    legal and regulatory aspects, 404.1
    tax accounting, 404.2
  brokers
    financial accounting, 405.3
    generally, 405
    legal and regulatory aspects, 405.1
    tax accounting, 405.2
  generally, 401
  subfranchising arrangements
    financial accounting, 402.3
    generally, 402
    legal and regulatory aspects, 402.1
    tax accounting, 402.2

National Bellas Hess, Inc. vs. Illinois Department of Revenue, 803
Nexus
  state and local income tax nexus. *See* State and local income tax nexus
  state sales and use tax nexus. *See* State sales and use tax nexus

Passive royalty income, 601
Personal holding companies
  case law, 602.3, 602.4
  compensation for services vs. royalty income, 602.4
  generally, 602
  legislative purpose and history, 602.2
  recommendations, 602.5
  statutory requirements, 602.1
Pooled advertising funds. *See* Advertising funds
Product and trade name franchises, 101

Retirement programs
  franchisor-sponsored programs for franchise owners, 1004
Royalties
  generally, 203
  passive losses from royalty arrangements, 1008
  S corporation passive royalty income, 603
  super-royalty provision on transfers to foreign entities, 902.1
  transfers, 303.3

Sales and disclosure
  FTC franchise disclosure rule, 106.1
  individual franchise sales, 303.1

regulation of
FTC franchise disclosure rule, 106.1
generally, 106
state regulatory activity, 106.2
S corporations
passive royalty income, 603
Section 1060
allocation of consideration under the residual method, 310.2
generally, 310
legislative history, 310.1
required reporting and compliance, 310.3
Section 6166, 1107
Seven-up Company, 502.1
State and local income tax nexus
background, 701
commerce clause, 703
due process, 702
generally, 708
multi-state tax commission, 707
New Mexico
engaging in business, 705.1
generally, 705
leasing property, 705.2
New York
allocation formula, 704.4
doing business, 704.1
employing capital, 704.3
generally, 704
jurisdiction, 704.2
South Carolina, 706
State sales and use tax nexus
generally, 801, 806
National Bellas Hess, Inc. vs. Illinois Department of Revenue, 803
problems
franchise fees, 804.2
generally, 804
services, 804.1
requirements, 802
taxable components of fees paid under franchising arrangements, 805
Subfranchising arrangements
multiple-unit transactions. *See* Multiple-unit transactions
Succession planning
generally, 1101
income tax liabilities, potential, 1106
Section 6166, availability of, 1107
transfer
overfunding the marital share, 1104
permission to, 1103
restrictions on, 1102
spouse, to, 1104
valuation
case law, 1105.3
empirical studies, 1105.1
generally, 1105
statutory changes, 1105.2

Targeted jobs tax credit programs, 1002
Tax accounting
area development agreements, 403.2
area representative agreements, 404.2
brokers, 405.2
subfranchising arrangements, 402.2
Tax planning considerations, 1001
Territorial agreements, 206.1
Transfers
Canterbury vs. Commissioner. See Canterbury vs. Commissioner
characterization and recognition of receipts by franchisor
generally, 303
individual franchise sales, 303.1
initial franchise fees, 303.2
license fees, 303.3
master license fees, 303.4
royalties, 303.3
service fees, 303.3
subsequent transfer fees, 303.5
deductibility of franchise costs by franchises
generally, 304
initial franchise fees, 304.2, 304.1.1, 304.1.2
present discounted value of right to deduct initial franchise fee, 304.2
different treatment of franchisor and franchisee, 305
fees
characterization and recognition of receipts by franchisor, 303.5
deductibility of franchise costs by franchises, 304.4
generally, 301
legislative history, 302
overriding royalty, 306
purchase of existing franchise operations at premium, 308
Section 1060. *See* Section 1060
succession planning
permission to transfer, 1103
restrictions, 1102
spouse, transfers to, 1104
unbundling of initial franchise fees, 307

ZEESOP, 1005
ZSOP, 1005